The Arnold and Caroline Rose Monog
of the American Sociological Associa

Juvenile delinquency and its origins

An integrated theoretical approach

Other books in the series

J. Milton Yinger, Kiyoshi Ikeda, Frank Laycock, and Stephen J. Cutler: *Middle Start: An Experiment in the Education Enrichment of Young Adolescents*

James A. Geschwender: *Class, Race, and Worker Insurgency: The League of Revolutionary Black Workers*

Paul Ritterband: *Education, Employment, and Migration: Israel in Comparative Perspective*

John Low-Beer: *Protest and Participation: The New Working Class in Italy*

Orrin E. Klapp: *Opening and Closing: Strategies of Information Adaptation in Society*

Rita James Simon: *Continuity and Change: A Study of Two Ethnic Communities in Israel*

Marshall B. Clinard: *Cities with Little Crime: The Case of Switzerland*

Steven T. Bossert: *Tasks and Social Relationships in Classrooms: A Study of Instructional Organization and Its Consequences*

David R. Heise: *Understanding Events: Affect and the Construction of Social Action*

Volumes previously published by the American Sociological Association

Michael Schwartz and Sheldon Stryker: *Deviance, Selves and Others*

Robert M. Hauser: *Socioeconomic Background and Educational Performance*

Morris Rosenberg and Roberta G. Simmons: *Black and White Self-Esteem: The Urban School Child*

Chad Gordon: *Looking Ahead: Self-Conceptions: Race and Family as Determinants of Adolescent Orientation to Achievement*

Anthony M. Orum: *Black Students in Protest: A Study of the Origins of the Black Student Movement*

Ruth M. Gasson, Archibald O. Haller, and William H. Sewell: *Attitudes and Facilitation in the Attainment of Status*

Sheila R. Klatzky: *Patterns of Contact with Relatives*

Herman Turk: *Interorganizational Activation in Urban Communities: Deductions from the Concept of System*

John DeLamater: *The Study of Political Commitment*

Alan C. Kerckhoff: *Ambition and Attainment: A Study of Four Samples of American Boys*

Scott McNall: *The Greek Peasant*

Lowell L. Hargens: *Patterns of Scientific Research: A Comparative Analysis of Research in Three Scientific Fields*

Charles Hirschman: *Ethnic Stratification in Peninsular Malaysia*

Juvenile delinquency and its origins

An integrated theoretical approach

Richard E. Johnson

Assistant Professor of Sociology
Brigham Young University

Cambridge University Press

Cambridge
London New York Melbourne

Published by the Syndics of the Cambridge University Press
The Pitt Building, Trumpington Street, Cambridge CB2 1RP
Bentley House, 200 Euston Road, London NW1 2DB
32 East 57th Street, New York, NY 10022, USA
296 Beaconsfield Parade, Middle Park, Melbourne 3206, Australia

First published 1979

Printed in the United States of America
Typeset by Telecki Publishing Services, 97 Bond Avenue, Malverne, NY 11565
Printed and bound by The Murray Printing Company, Westford, Mass.

Library of Congress Cataloging in Publication Data

Johnson, Richard E. 1949–
Juvenile delinquency and its origins

(The Arnold and Caroline Rose monograph series
of the American Sociological Association)

Bibliography: p.

1. Juvenile delinquency. 2. Criminal behavior, Prediction of.
I. Title. II. Series: The Arnold and Caroline Rose
monograph series in sociology.
HV9069.J57 364.36 78-67263
ISBN 0 521 22477 2 hard covers
ISBN 0 521 29516 5 paperback

Contents

Figures

Tables

1. Major theoretical perspectives on juvenile delinquency

The past half century of sociological research on juvenile delinquency has led to the development of a diversity of causal images in the search for an understanding of the phenomenon. Moreover, the tendency has been to set up each major theoretical orientation against the others to determine which of the competing theories is "true" in a given research setting. These competing perspectives have been categorized in a number of ways (as a perusal of any sample of textbook contents will reveal), but the focus here is upon three major theoretical orientations known as strain theory, subculture theory, and control theory (cf. Hirschi, 1969:3–15). Each entails a different conception of how adolescents become delinquent.

This study, however, is based on the assumption that each orientation has pinpointed certain processes that play a role in generating delinquent behavior. The either/or approach of many researchers is rejected in favor of drawing together the most useful and empirically tenable features of the major theories, incorporating them into a coherent conception of delinquency causation to be represented in a causal model, and testing the empirical tenability of the resulting model.

This chapter briefly reviews the causal images contained in these three orientations. Specifically, it explores the implications of the major perspectives for specific issues in delinquency causation. These center around the roles of social class, family, school, perceptions of the future, peer associations, personal values, and the deterrent effect of perceived risk of apprehension in producing or discouraging delinquency. These special topics will be discussed following a brief overview of the general theoretical stances.

The key to any *strain* explanation of adolescent law violation (Merton, 1938; Cohen, 1955; Cloward and Ohlin, 1960) is the proposition that some adolescents are driven to law violation in response to the frustration of experiencing or anticipating failure. The pressure to deviate from acceptable behavior norms is created by a discrepancy between culturally induced aspirations and realistic expectations. The individual internalizes the goals of society but must employ illegitimate means to obtain them when legitimate avenues to success are blocked. The causal image is the same whether the frustration or lack of opportunity involves economic success goals (Merton, 1938) or adolescent peer group status (Cohen, 1955). The frustrated, deprived, or strained individual violates society's rules to obtain the commodities that society has convinced him or her are important to obtain.

The defining characteristic of a *subculture* perspective is the view of an adolescent as drawn or socialized into law violation in an attempt to live up to the perceived expectations of his or her deviant associates. Whereas individual subculture theories (Cohen, 1955; Cloward and Ohlin, 1960; Miller, 1958; Sutherland and Cressey, 1974; Akers, 1973) vary a great deal in terminology and focus, they all share the common element of stressing "affiliational" (cf. Matza, 1969) causal processes. Deviance is seen as adherence to the norms, expectations, or definitions of one's associates, which happen to differ from the prevailing norms, expectations, and definitions of the dominant society.

Both strain and subculture orientations are essentially motivational theories (Briar and Piliavin, 1965) in which the disposition to deviate (*a*) derives from certain interpersonal or social conditions, (*b*) is essentially a permanent aspect of the personality or value framework of the individual, and (*c*) propels the person into illegal behavior.

The third major orientation - *control* theory - is not concerned with delinquency-causing motivations or provocations but rather with factors that prevent deviance (Nye, 1958; Hirschi, 1969; Hewitt, 1970; Briar and Piliavin, 1965; Toby, 1957; Karacki and Toby, 1962; Polk and Halferty, 1966). Each adolescent develops a degree of commitment to (or stake in) conformity through the formation of social bonds to aspects of conventional society. Hirschi (1969), for example, specifies that the prospects of delinquent behavior decline as the adolescent is controlled by such bonds as affective ties to parents, success in school, involvement in school activities, high occupational and educational aspirations, and belief in the moral validity of conventional norms. To the control theorist, the delinquent act is the result not of being drawn or driven but rather of being freed from constraints.

As compared with explanations centered on strain or on subcultures, the control perspective emphasizes irrational and situational aspects of deviant acts. As Schrag (1971:109) points out, control theories "focus attention on the dynamics of the interactional processes by which people move towards and beyond the brink of deviant behavior . . . [A] deliberate and autonomous decision to commit an act of crime, followed by an appropriate sequence of responses leading to the act, is an uncommon occurrence."

The discussion to this point has entailed only brief, general descriptions of the theories. Their various implications regarding the roles of certain key variables in the causation of delinquent behavior are discussed here.

Social class

On the authority of the pioneering research of Shaw and McKay (1942) and of official crime statistics in general, it was long accepted as fact that the relative incidence of delinquent behavior varied by social class. However, the major theoretical orientations differ in their presumptions about the relation between social class and delinquent behavior.

Strain theory was, in effect, created to account for the "fact" that delinquency and adult crime are more common among lower-class individuals. Merton's discussion (1938), though perhaps centered around adult criminal behavior, contains the following suggestions regarding adolescent law violations, which are the focus of the present study:

1. Aspirations are approximately the same in all social classes.
2. Expectations are reduced among lower-class adolescents because of their disadvantages in the competition for educational, occupational, and economic success.
3. The pressure toward delinquency is proportional to the discrepancy between aspirations and expectations.
4. Delinquent behavior is therefore primarily a lower-class phenomenon.

Cloward and Ohlin (1960) share this same presumption of greater lower-class deviance, and they extend the analysis to include opportunities for various kinds of illegal activities as another important variable in determining specific delinquent responses.

Cohen's "status deprivation" version of strain theory likewise attempts to explain greater amounts of lower-class delinquency (1955:26, 30, 42 ff.). He sees virtually all boys as aspiring to success in middle-class schools. Lower-class boys are at a disadvantage in doing well because of deficient socialization and the school's "middle-class bias," and thus they experience status frustration or strain – often resulting in a "reaction formation" against their own middle-class values. Delinquent gangs of lower-class boys form as a collective solution to shared frustrations.

At this point in his explanation of gang delinquency, Cohen may be classified as a subculture theorist, in that the gang is said to develop a set of norms prescribing delinquent behavior. His gangs are more properly "contracultures," in that they exhibit negativistic, malicious, and nonutilitarian behavior, directly flaunting conventional expectations. But the essential ingredient is that delinquency is seen as conformity to separate norms.

As a general perspective, subculture theory as defined herein does not imply a necessary relation between class and delinquency. Sutherland's notion of differential association, for example, applies to definitions conducive to law violation in any stratum of society. For historical reasons, however, subcultural norms and values conducive to delinquent behavior are presumed to flourish primarily among the lower class.

Walter Miller (1958) is a prime exponent of the view that a separate lower-class subculture in America is built around a set of "focal concerns" that differ significantly from those of the middle class. In his words, middle class and lower class "are to an important degree different worlds, with different emphases, different values, different bases of concern, and different definitions of reality" (Kvaraceus and Miller, 1959:59). Segalman (1965) likewise dichotomizes the middle class and the underclass according to basic views of American life.

From this outline of the subcultural perspective, the following implications are evident:

1. Delinquency is conformity to norms.
2. Middle-class and lower-class youths have different norms, values, and aspirations.
3. Delinquency is primarily a lower-class occurrence, as middle-class norms prevail in that part of society which is given authority to define delinquency and to label the offender.

Neither strain theory nor subculture theory offers much in the way of an explanation of middle-class delinquency. The paucity of work in this area is probably the result of the fact that official records show a concentration of juvenile delinquency in the lower socioeconomic levels. Cloward and Ohlin are described as holding "a personality explanation for most middle-class delinquency" (Miller, 1970:40). Cohen, too, holds that middle-class delinquency results primarily from a boy's lack of identification with his father, followed by rebellious behavior aimed at proving his masculinity (1955:162–9; see also Parsons, 1947). He adds that this problem of male role identification is greatest for middle-class boys in industrial society (1955:164–6). Later Cohen suggests that the apparent increase in middle-class delinquency in recent years is the result of a weakening of the middle-class pattern of deferred gratification (see Vaz, 1967:203–7). Kvaraceus and Miller see middle-class delinquents as "disturbed" and lower-class delinquents as "normal." Hence, the common implication of these theories is not only that there is more delinquency in the lower class, but that qualitatively different processes lead to delinquent behavior, depending on social class position.

The implication from both strain and subculture theories is that the frequency, the seriousness, and even the basic patterns or types of delinquent behavior should vary by social class position. Control theorists, on the other hand, commonly make no assumption about the relative strength of social controls or bonds in different social classes, and hence make no class-related claims. This approach has resulted in part from the development of self-report techniques of measuring delinquent behavior and the consequent questioning of the causal role of social class.[1] The more recently developed control formulations therefore encountered no presumed "fact" of a social class influence on delinquency to explain.

The family

Very few explicit hypotheses about the role of parental factors in delinquency causation are deducible from strain or subculture theories. This is no surprise in view of the macro or structural level of analysis of these orientations. Most versions of these perspectives were never intended to predict which individuals would become involved in delinquency, but merely which sectors of society are most vulnerable to delinquency-producing influences. Subculture theory does imply, however, that deviant parents will produce delinquent offspring.

Assertions about the effects of intrafamilial, "under-the-roof" experiences on delinquency are left largely to the control perspective. The central theme is that the more satisfying the parent–child relationship, the less likely it is that the child will deviate. This presumes that the parent stands for conformity, so that the child has a meaningful relationship to lose or damage by deviating from parental expectations.

The school

All three of the major orientations assign some relevance to the role of the school in generating delinquent behavior. Within the strain formulation, the school is the setting in which frustrations are most sharply felt. Economic success in adulthood, as well as immediate success in the adolescent social world, are highly dependent upon school success. Negative experiences in school produce a lowering of expectations, a heightened sense of strain, and the consequent projection into delinquent activities.

The subculture orientation cannot ignore the importance of school success to adult success in American society. One of the crucial value differences between the middle class and the lower class cited in formulations such as Miller's is a lesser degree of commitment to education by the latter. In a sense the relationship between educational commitment and delinquency in this theory is a spurious correlation. By following their own distinct values and focal concerns, lower-class adolescents become more delinquent and less committed to education simultaneously.

Control theory, of course, stresses the roles of attachments to teachers, positive experiences in school activities, and desires or plans for future educational success as factors that act to decrease delinquency through increasing the adolescent's stake in conformity. A school failure has little to lose by being caught in a delinquent act; a school success risks losing both current rewarding experiences and future educational and occupational opportunities.

Perceptions of the future

It is clear that strain theory is the most future oriented of the major perspectives. In fact, aspirations, expectations, and the discrepancy between them (strain) are all present feelings about future hopes and possibilities. It is the calculation of the yet-to-be that sparks the frustration in the mind of the lower-class youth, who sees his or her chances for success blocked at every turn. Thus it follows that aspiring to a future of wealth and status – "the American Dream" – can become a key element in the processes generating illegal behavior.

Subculture theorists are generally mute on the effects of perceptions of the future in the etiology of delinquency. They rarely tread beyond that point in the immediate future at which delinquent responses are expected to receive approval from delinquent associates.

Control theory is typically present oriented, with its emphasis on situational factors and current social bonds. As Briar and Piliavin state: "Younger boys, those in the age group with the highest rate of delinquent behavior, are not affected by job market conditions; rather, their behavior is influenced, as we have argued above, by more mundane situational considerations" (1965:290–1).

When control theorists do venture into the world of future perceptions, they come up with somewhat different predictions than do strain theorists. As Hirschi (1969:170–1) points out, higher educational or occupational aspirations should act as important controlling linkages to society, regardless of the corresponding levels of realistic expectations. Expectations of success should also act as controls against deviation, independently of wishful desires.

Delinquent associates

Traditional subculture theory places highest emphasis on the influence of group pressures in generating delinquency. Cohen (1955) and Cloward and Ohlin (1960) suggest that delinquents have been socialized within cohesive delinquent groups to hold attitudes and values conducive to antilegal behavior. Similarly, Miller (1958) asserts that the focal concerns of the adolescent corner groups are belonging and status – two key propellants into illegal acts committed to gain peer approval. And finally, the greater the association with delinquent others, the greater the likelihood of "differential association" with "definitions conducive to law violation" (Sutherland and Cressey, 1974).

Strain theory in its early form (Merton, 1938) accorded no explicit theoretical relevance to group pressures, but in its subsequent formulations (Cohen, 1955; Cloward and Ohlin, 1960) strain is presumed to be the source of delinquent peer groups that in turn encourage delinquent acts. Indeed, Cohen's "status deprivation" conception pinpoints status striving within the delinquent gang as a key motive in flaunting society's rules.

Control theory, in its purest form (Hirschi, 1969), accords no importance to the pull of delinquent associates. The same lack of social bonds that generates delinquency also facilitates associations with other delinquents, creating a spurious correlation between delinquent associates and delinquent behavior. However, Hirschi concludes that he initially underestimated the causal influence of delinquent associates. Moreover, other control theorists recognize that part of the general motivation to break legal rules (which must therefore be controlled) is "to portray courage in the presence of, or be loyal to peers" (Briar and Piliavin, 1965:36).

Delinquent values

Each of the major orientations places some significance upon personal values as influencing the likelihood of delinquency. As stated above, strict subculture theorists like Miller (1958), and Cohen (1955) to a lesser extent, depict American values as sharply dichotomized between middle class and "working" (lower) class. No one really acts against personal values; the values just happen to differ. Thus all delinquents should believe in the appropriateness of their delinquent acts.

Merton (1938), by contrast, posits the virtually universal acceptance of traditional American middle-class values. A great frustration or strain is necessary to induce someone to break through a portion of his or her own value system (legitimate norms) in the attempt to fulfill another portion (cultural goals) of those same values.

Control theorists generally include some sort of "internal control" (Nye, 1958:7) or conscience, or "belief in the moral validity of social norms" (Hirschi, 1969), as one of their deviance-preventing mechanisms. As such, they imply a continuum of individual degrees of acceptance of values consonant with delinquent actions. Moreover, they recognize the possibility of "drift" from (Matza, 1964), or "neutralization" of (Sykes and Matza, 1957), personal moral constraints. Again, the picture of delinquency is much more situational from a control viewpoint.

Deterrence

Although sociological theories of delinquency causation have not emphasized the fear of apprehension as a deterrent to delinquent involvement, there is a large body of literature focusing on deterrence (cf. Johnson, 1974, or Gibbs, 1975, for a summary; see also Kandle, 1974). The general image of control theory is more compatible with the assumption of a deterrent effect of perceived risk of official apprehension than is the image of either strain theory or subculture theory. Briar and Piliavin (1965), for example, include "fear of deprivations and punishment" as part of their conception of "commitment to conformity." But control theory has commonly emphasized a different kind of deterrent effect – restraint from deviance because of the likelihood of its visibility to close associates who would disapprove and because of the negative implications of categorization as delinquent for institutional ties and future success chances.

Subculture theory, on the other hand, seems to entail the implicit presumption that the approval of delinquent associates will outweigh any potential negative consequences of official apprehension. And strain theory seems to entail the implicit presumption that the risk of official apprehension will not deter because delinquency is seen either as an instrumentally effective adaptation to blocked legitimate opportunities or as an irrational adaptation to the frustration of finding instrumental channels blocked.

Summary

These descriptions of strain, subculture, and control statements and implications are not intended to be detailed summaries. They serve two main purposes. First, they focus the reader's attention on the general positions of the major theories concerning the relevance of several key variables in sociologists' search for causes of delinquent behavior. Second, even this brief look at these orientations should convince the reader of the complexity of the issues and of the futility of attempting to demonstrate which theory is "true." In some cases the theories predict the same associations; in other areas opposite relationships are implied; and on the influences of certain variables, one or more of the theories may simply be silent. And, of course, this list by no means covers the range of possibly relevant variables in delinquency causation.

Having gained an appreciation for complexity and a flavoring of the major hypotheses, the reader can now more fruitfully proceed to the review of past studies in Chapter 2. The intent is to select those aspects of each of the major perspectives that remain tenable under the scrutiny of empirical evidence. Then, in Chapter 3, the pieces will be put together with even further theoretical and empirical contributions in the form of a causal model of delinquent behavior.

2. What others have found: a review of the data

It would be foolhardy to attempt to assess the weight of all the evidence regarding the etiology of delinquency within the confines of this study. At the outset, the discussion is limited to theoretical propositions that are sociological or social psychological in nature. Certain biological or psychological factors undoubtedly play a role in generating delinquent conduct by some adolescents at some times. However, as general explanations they seem to lack empirical support. To quote Gibbons (1976:73), "The many years of biogenic exploration of delinquency have not produced any valid generalizations about biological factors in deviance." Furthermore, "analysis has rejected psychoanalytic claims and notions about psychopathy as untestable" (p. 87). And finally, "The mass of studies which have searched for these severe emotional disturbances have failed to find them. In short, it appears that delinquents are no more or less ridden with personality pathology than are nonoffenders" (p. 87).

The review of the data in this chapter will be confined to studies bearing on the issues cited in the previous chapter. The goal is to determine which claims of which major orientations are refuted or supported by studies exploring the relationships of delinquent behavior with social class, intrafamilial relationships, school experiences, conceptions of future opportunities, delinquent peer associations, delinquent personal values, and perceived risk of apprehension. Certain decisions are made in this chapter, on the basis of a review of past studies, concerning which variables to retain as part of a causal model of adolescents' law violations. These decisions do not represent the present study's conclusions. Rather, the present aim is to determine which variables and propositions to include for further testing with new data.

Social class

As previously indicated, strain and subculture theories predict an inverse relationship between socioeconomic status (SES) and delinquent behavior. Control theory does not. This divergence has set the stage for what many have considered a crucial test between class-based propositions and all others.

Official statistics from police and court records do indeed support the claim that delinquency is disproportionately exhibited by lower-class adolescents. However, delinquency is reduced from a variable to an attribute by the use of official statistics. Moreover, it is an attribute confounded by inconsistent police and court responses to similar deviant acts. Official statistics are therefore more useful in examining society's reaction to delinquent acts than in seeking explanations for delinquency as a behavioral variable.

The class theories to be tested predict a differential distribution of delinquent acts caused by variable pressures and norms. They remain silent regarding the official labeling of delinquent behavior (Cloward and Ohlin, 1960: 3). For these reasons it seems preferable to use self-report data, which "makes possible a 'true' incidence of deviation" (Dentler and Monroe, 1961:733), rather than relying upon probably biased official records. The picture of American delinquent behavior from the two types of data can vary markedly (see, for example, Williams and Gold, 1972).

The major flaw in self-report studies, however, is that the legal definitions of delinquency are often disregarded. Mere deviance from ideals should not be equated with delinquency, best defined "by acts, the detection of which is thought to result in punishment of the person committing them by agents of the larger society" (Hirschi, 1969:47), or simply by "chargeability" (Gold, 1966). As Voss has rightly noted, "unless differences regarding definition are recognized, future research will continue to produce contradictory results" (Gold and Voss, 1967: 120). Yet self-report studies, and especially those employing statutory definitions of delinquency, are still the most valid tests of the theories. The specific problems of reliability and validity of this methodology are widely discussed (see, for example, Hood and Sparks, 1970:64–70) and need not be reiterated here, The issue will be discussed in more detail in Chapter 4.

The present question is whether there is reason to expect systematic differences in reliability or validity according to the SES of respondents. It appears doubtful that there is sufficient distortion of the findings from forgetfulness, dishonesty, and nonattendance at school testing sites to bias the results relevant to socioeconomic status significantly (see Hirschi, 1969: 54–65). Martin Gold (1966:30) disagrees in part, stating that anonymouns self-report questionnaires (as opposed to self-report interviews yield an overreporting of trivial offenses by higher-SES youths.

In actual findings, however, Gold's (1966) elimination of this excessive reported delinquency by higher SES youths through careful interviewing does not result in a striking relationship between SES and delinquency. He finds only a slight negative relationship (and for boys only), which accounts for no more than 4 percent of the variance. Erickson and Empey get similar results, concluding that class is "really a poor predictor of delinquency" (1965:272). Another study claiming to find the relationship predicted by class theories (Reiss and Rhodes, 1961) is not comparable, in that it employs both self-report and official data to label boys delinquent or nondelinquent. Other studies that find more delinquency in the lower class include MacDonald (1969) and Gold (1963), who use semiofficial police contacts to measure delinquency.

On the other hand, "careful quantitative research shows again and again that the relation between socioeconomic status and the commission of delinquent acts is small, or nonexistent" (Hirschi, 1969:66). Concurrence with and empirical support for this view abound in the literature, including tests for both boys and girls, for various community sizes, for numerous types of offenses, and for diverse locations (Nye, Short, and Olson, 1958; Dentler and Monroe, 1961; Clark and Wenninger, 1962; Slocum and Stone, 1963; Akers, 1964; Nye, 1958; Porterfield, 1943; Porterfield and Clifton, 1946; Himelhoch, 1964; Pine, 1965; Gibbens and Ahrenfeldt, 1966; Stinchcombe, 1964; Voss, 1966; Jessor et al., 1968; Berger and Simon, 1974; Williams and Gold, 1972; Kelly and Pink, 1973 and 1975; Frease, 1973; Weis, 1973:415; Arnold, 1965; Vaz, 1966).

Most of these same studies also support the view that the vast majority of American adolescents commit at least one chargeable offense (see Williams and Gold, 1972, who found 88 percent of a national sample so reporting). Yet most youths do not progress to very serious or very repetitive offending patterns (cf. Wolfgang et al., 1972:244–55; Hood and Sparks, 1970:46–63). Delinquent behavior so extensive yet episodic does not support the images in strain and subculture formulations of certain disadvantaged youth being driven or drawn into careers of deviation.

Given that the frequency of delinquency is relatively evenly distributed along the SES scales, proponents of class views insist that the type of offense varies systematically by SES. The President's Commission on

Law Enforcement and Administration of Justice does not doubt that "especially the most serious delinquency, is committed disproportionately by slum and lower-class youth" (in Voss, 1970:12–17). Gibbons (1976:38) echoes the relatively common belief that "evidence indicates that the more serious, actionable offenses are more frequent among persons of lower socioeconomic status, hence referral rates are higher for those individuals." Indeed, self-reports in some cases correlate highly with official court records supposedly "biased against the lower class" (Erickson, 1972). And courts are presumed to direct their attention toward more serious offenses.

A few self-report studies do find more serious delinquency among lower-class youth, but the issue seems complicated by the matter of neighborhood or area of residence. Clark and Wenninger (1962) report no relationships between SES and delinquency in rural and small-town settings but find more delinquency reported by lower-class adolescents who live in large, homogeneous lower-class urban areas. Voss (1966) reports a similar finding of variation in admitted delinquency by school districts or neighborhoods, but not by SES within areas. Yet Hirschi (1969) reports little or no relation between the socioeconomic status of an area and its rate of self-reported delinquency (p. 70), though it is doubtful that any of his areas fits the description of a homogeneous lower-class (slum) neighborhood.

Perhaps the central line of argument by those who believe offenses to be more serious in lower SES groups is the contention that self-report schedules are often so loaded with "nuisance offenses" (of which lower SES youths are *not* presumed to be disproportionately guilty) that the results overestimate the amount of middle-class delinquency. Indeed, the point is well taken in some instances. For example, Nye and Short (1956:328) purposely selected items that would be "committed by an appreciable segment of the population" in attempting to scale delinquent behavior. They included defying parents' authority, skipping school, and driving without a license. Because these forms of deviance are undoubtedly widespread, they may tend to distort or mask unobserved SES differences in "real" delinquent behavior.

The objection against nuisance offenses does not hold in all cases, however. Hirschi (1969:54) defines delinquency in terms of six legally punishable acts (for adults as well as juveniles). Moreover, seriousness is also checked by questions dealing with frequency of offenses and the possibility of reform (1969:56). Even with such a carefully constructed definition of delinquency, Hirschi finds little or no evidence of a relationship between SES and delinquency (1969:69). Gold (1966), too, checks for seriousness, employing very careful methods, and finds only a slight relationship.

Empey (1967) has concluded that the seriousness of delinquent acts is not related to SES. Yet the evidence here is not as convincing as that documenting the frequency of delinquent acts. Gold's (1966) warning that anonymous overreporting of trivia may lead to an overestimate of delinquency among high-SES youth must be recognized. Moreover, officially institutionalized delinquents have been found to be more serious self-report offenders than their noninstitutionalized peers (Hood and Sparks, 1970:58; Short and Nye, 1958). Because relatively more of these official delinquents are lower class, samples drawn from noninstitutionalized populations would tend to reveal too little seriousness of lower-class delinquency. Although such qualifications reduce the argument against class-related theories, the overall effect remains that there is very little direct support for these theories in the available self-report data.

Adding to this conclusion the observations that there is "little to distinguish" middle SES and lower SES delinquent groups in organizational structure, ingredients and motivations, solidarity, and conflict with other groups (Bloch and Niederhoffer, 1958:7–9), and that delinquency in both middle and lower SES is peer oriented (Reiss and Rhodes, 1961) and similar in the proportion of offenses committed in the company of peers (Erickson, 1973), further doubt is cast on class theories that imply distinct delinquency-producing processes. There is, of course, the possibility that different causal chains operate in the different social classes to yield similar patterns of delinquent activity, but it seems safe to conclude that "social class by itself may be a poor clue to delinquency" (Empey, 1967:32). Perhaps "consistency requires that 'socioeconomic status' be removed from the dictionary of delinquency theory and research" (Hirschi, 1969:67). However, it is easy to concur with Hirschi's uneasiness about disassociating the concepts of social position and delinquent behavior.

The nagging fact is that "Nearly all authorities agree that persistent organized, gang forms of juvenile misconduct are concentrated in working-class neighborhoods (urban core slums)" (Gibbons, 1976:115). So there is no clear verdict on the role of class in delinquency. The socioeconomic status of an adolescent appears to be relatively unimportant, yet the class of his or her neighborhood – especially if it happens to be a large lower-class sector – seems to play a role in generating at least gang-type delinquency.

Questionable research methods may be one contributor to these somewhat unexpected findings. The most distressing point about the testing of class theories is well stated by Hirschi (1969:71):

> the *class* model implicit in most theories of delinquency is a peculiarly top-heavy, two-class model made up of the overwhelming majority of respectable people on the one hand and the lumpenproletariat on the other. The *stratification* model used by delinquency researchers is another thing . . . the group the delinquency theorists have had in mind may not be well represented, if it is represented at all.

In other words, studies based on in-school populations may not include the "lumpenproletariat" or theoretical lower class. Schoenberg (1975), for example, could not include "family economic pathology" variables in his secondary analysis of self-report data, as the variances were too small to obtain reliable estimates. Even when the theorists' lower class is sampled, its members are likely to lose their distinct identity when respondents are stratified by SES according to father's occupation. Thus a major problem in testing class theories seems to be the lack of adequate operational definitions of the lower class.

Subculture theorists Cohen and Miller seem to ignore SES and to define the lower class tautologically. Cohen speaks of economically middle-class families producing delinquency because they are really lower class culturally (1955:158–9). Likewise, Kvaraceus and Miller (1959) speak of middle-class delinquents as really exhibiting "lower class conduct," explaining away middle-class delinquency by redefining it as lower class. If social class is defined in terms of delinquent behavior, there is no point in arguing that class explains delinquency. It would be more appropriate to substitute "futuristic" versus "present" orientation, or other such value differences, for what Kvaraceus and Miller call "middle class" and "lower class." These authors frankly admit that wealth is "becoming less useful as a primary determinant of family status" (1959: 62). Instead of predicting relationships between class and delinquency, therefore, the subculture orientation seems more concerned with relationships between different value orientations and delinquency. If so, it is meaningless to evaluate the theory according to father's occupation or other SES data.

Strain theory, by contrast, implies a socioeconomic rather than valuational definition of class. The problem here is one of deciding where to draw the line on SES scales to separate the lower and middle classes consistently with the theoretical formulations. Once again, the criteria for defining lower class are vague. Researchers have most frequently turned to father's occupation as the indicator, because there is much evidence for its validity and reliability as an index of position along the SES continuum (Hirschi, 1969:69–70). It is an easy indicator to administer in a questionnaire, and the addition of other measures, such as father's or mother's education, does not alter the relationship between SES and delinquent behavior (Dentler and Monroe, 1961:736; Hirschi, 1969:75). Using father's occupation, most definitions of social class employed in research are stepladders of occupational types.

The difficulty is that these measures of social class, often including more than one category as a composite lower class, have very little in common with the implied (or explicit) theoretical definitions. And any one lowest category (blue collar, unskilled labor, etc.) undoubtedly includes some economically secure union workers who would not be expected to experience lower-class strain, along with those who are truly destitute.

It is doubtful that *any* father's occupation scale (even one dividing "lower class" from "the rest" as consistently as possible with strain theory) can serve effectively in testing class theories of delinquency. Many members of the theoretical lower class are likely to be neglected as not classifiable if the father is unemployed or absent. Dentler and Monroe (1961), for example, found 27 percent of their sample not classifiable by father's occupation. It seems unlikely that this proportion of the sample would be randomly distributed by social class. For these reasons there is a need for a refined conceptualization of social class before class propositions can be adequately tested.

Gunnar Myrdal (see Heller, 1969:138–43) has observed in America an "underclass" that seems very close to the delinquency theorists' lower class. He describes this class as "not really an integrated part of the nation but a useless and miserable substratum." Members of the underclass are uneducated outcasts who "become unemployed, and indeed largely unemployable or underemployed." The underclass is the poverty class, the slum class, the class of "utter destitution." Consistent with strain theory, Myrdal's underclass is characterized by very limited opportunity, yet it is not defined by father's occupation or the like. The definition is a constellation of such factors as unemployment or marginal employment, family disorganization, low level of schooling or training, and absolute poverty income.

John Hewitt (1970) appears to recognize this underclass as his lower class and cites its special relevance to delinquency. Characteristics of Hewitt's lower class include female head of household, marginal or no employment, poverty-level income, and receipt of welfare benefits (1970:55–7, 69). He characterizes lower-class life as guided more by coercive and situational demands than by positive norms. Absolute and relative deprivation are the rule, and daily problems include the problem of survival. It is a picture of a social class not very different from that implied by traditional strain theory. Cohen (1955), for example, describes his so-called working class with terms such as "needy" and "underpriviledged" (p. 26), "poverty" (p. 40), and "slum areas" (p. 43).

More fruitful tests of class-delinquency theories would employ the concept of underclass and replace father's occupation with indicators such as father's marginal employment or unemployment, and destitution (poverty-level income and receipt of welfare benefits). So measured, social class may indeed prove to be substantially related to self-reported delinquent behavior.

Such a view of the underclass, however, suggests that there are some basic delinquency-relevant similarities among members of the remainder of society. There is a line of thought in stratification theory consistent with the combining of virtually all regular earners. Exemplified by C. Wright Mills (1951), this tradition includes the notions of the "proletarianization of the middle class" and the "bourgeoisification of the working class." Mills's basic thesis is that there is an increasing leveling of the various portions of the "earning class" in social stratification. Kurt Mayer (1963:467–8) agrees that designations such as working class versus middle class "are losing their validity . . . many people hold different positions in the various rank orders." He sees the situation as "so fluid that one can no longer speak of classes in the middle ranges."

There is some empirical evidence of such a melding of the earning class. Bloch and Niederhoffer observed twenty years ago that "the accepted distinctions between the two classes (lower and middle by father's occupation) are breaking down. Status differentials based on salary, residence and education are fast disappearing" (1958:177–8). Census Bureau (1963) statistics show that in 1960 the median income for craftsmen (blue collar) exceeded that for sales or clerical workers (white collar). Blau (1957) found that the average "skilled occupation" rated above the average "white-collar" occupation on the National Opinion Research Center prestige scale of occupations. Reiss et al. (1961:157), noting the overlap between white-collar and manual occupations on that same scale, concluded that little is added to the analysis by making a distinction between these categories of workers. Finally, Hodge et al. (in Heller, 1969:198–9) contend that "one can see the appreciable overlap in scores between professional, other white-collar, and blue-collar occupations. Although these divisions are often employed by social scientists as though they represented fundamental class barriers . . . no such barrier can be detected on the basis of occupational prestige."

It is unreasonable to claim that blue-collar workers and white-collar workers in America enjoy identical life chances and life styles. Many observers caution against such dramatic conclusions (cf. Rinehart, 1971). Yet life chances are sufficiently similar among these "earners" – in contrast to the underclass – that the blue-collar/white-collar line should be dropped in the examination of class-related theories of delinquency. An underclass/earning-class line is more theoretically consistent.

It is noteworthy that at the opposite end of the SES continuum, another theoretically relevant line has recently been proposed by Weis (1973) between professional and managerial segments of the white-collar middle class. It is encouraging to see socioeconomic lines being drawn on theoretical rather than convenience grounds. Both of the studies (Hirschi, 1969; Douglas et al., 1966) cited by Weis in support of delinquency differences within the middle class also reveal differences within the working-class or blue-collar sector.

Hirschi's data support the importance of the underclass model to delinquency. Although he finds no relation between SES (father's occupation) and delinquency, his data "show that the boys whose fathers have been unemployed and/or whose families are on welfare are more likely than children from fully employed, self-sufficient families to commit delinquent acts" (1969:72).

The Douglas et al. (1966) data are less impressive, because they entail official statistics that could be biased against the underclass. But they nevertheless show that in Britain the difference between lower-middle-class (white-collar) and upper-manual-working-class (blue-collar) delinquency is nil, although there is much greater delinquency in the lower manual working class.

Several other self-report studies contain indirect empirical support for the separation of the underclass and earning class and the predicted relevance of that separation to delinquency. Hewitt (1970:77) points out that Short and Nye (1957) "found that only in their lowest stratum (corresponding roughly with our lower class) was there any evidence of a link between class and delinquency." Because Short and Nye's lowest stratum was an SES category undoubtedly including some nonunderclass respondents, the correlation would probably have been stronger for the underclass itself.

Finally, Gold's (1966:42–3) data are quite strikingly in accord with the predicted relevance of social class to delinquency, using the underclass conceptualization. His finding of a small negative relationship between SES and delinquency is not the result of a gradual increase in delinquency as one proceeds down the SES stepladder. Rather, the relationship results almost entirely from much greater delinquency by the lowest-status boys.

To balance the scales, however, it should be noted that Berger and Simon (1974), in a representative sample of the state of Illinois, defined low class in a manner not unlike the underclass conception and found no apparent effect on delinquency. Their low class – characterized by father's unemployment and consistently low father's education and occupation levels – admitted less delinquency than the higher working class in all race/sex subcategories.

Thus, whereas father's occupation or SES per se is of little utility in the explanation of delinquency, the concept of social class and the theories relating it to delinquency should not be prematurely discarded on the basis of available data. Though there does not appear to be great cause to expect class to arise as a prime general cause of American delinquent behavior, even if conceived in underclass/earning-class terms, other variables usually assumed to be correlates of lower-class membership – poverty, welfare, unemployment – appear to play some role in the causal scheme. Hence, the variable social class will be incorporated in the causal model to be tested.

The family

As stated in Chapter 1, the present concern with family factors is centered around the nature of the parent–child relationship. Control formulations predict that this bond will be the first if not foremost delinquency-preventing social linkage. The data tend to support the hypothesis. Hirschi (1969) finds delinquent behavior to increase with each of the following: lack of parental communication and sympathy, laxity of parental supervision, and absence of adult role models. Hindelang (1973) replicates these findings in a rural setting.

Nye's (1958) study is replete with various kinds of positive attachments to parents that are associated with less reported delinquency. Interestingly, he finds greater delinquency in unhappy intact homes than in simply broken homes (Nye, 1958:47), indicating the importance of the quality of parent–child relationships, as opposed to the mere presence of parents in the home.

Studies utilizing official delinquency reports (Glueck and Glueck, 1950), semiofficial police contacts (Gold, 1963), and self-reported norm violations of various kinds (Dentler and Monroe, 1961; Slocum and Stone, 1963; Miller and Simon, 1974; Schoenberg, 1975) all support the propositions that affection for and involvement with parents are associated with less delinquency. Even in the case of relatively rare "behavior problem" aggressive deviance, parental rejection seems to be the prime mover (Bandura and Walters, 1959; cf. Gibbons, 1976:194–201).

A second issue regarding parental influences on delinquency revolves around the question of the effects of parental deviance. Formulators of subculture theories from Walter Miller to Edwin Sutherland predict that deviant parents tend to socialize or reinforce deviance in their offspring. Thus an affective tie to a criminal parent would tend to lead to the child's adoption of the parent's nonconventional behavior patterns (by simple cognitive-balance-theory reasoning). In the real world, then, in order for parental ties to induce consistent conformity, either (*a*) all parents must conform or at least stand for conformity in the eyes of their children, or (*b*) children will be less likely to attach themselves to deviant parents. Both phenomena seem to occur in our society.

Even youths heavily involved in delinquency value conventional accomplishments more than they value success in delinquency (Short and Strodtbeck, 1965; Lerman, 1968). It follows that parental deviance will likewise attenuate the attraction of the child to the parent. Complementing these findings are data indicating that parents, even in high-crime neighborhoods, almost universally accept the larger society's values about the wrongness and seriousness of the most common juvenile offenses (Maccoby et al., 1958). And Hirschi's data (1969:97) lead him to conclude that "those lower-class boys committing delinquent acts are not finding support for their actions from their parents."

However, Hirschi's data on those boys whose parents receive welfare or are unemployed are not clear on this point (p. 96). Furthermore, the maxim that actions speak louder than words cannot be ignored. Parents may espouse conformity while modeling all kinds of manipulative, dishonest, violent, or destructive behavior in the presence of impressionable offspring (cf. Epstein, 1967).

In sum, the notion of parental deviance and/or socialization as a direct cause of delinquency has limited, but plausible, applicability. It does not seem to merit inclusion in a general model of delinquency causation on a par with parental attachment, but it certainly deserves at least tangential consideration.

The school

As all of the major theories accord some importance to negative school experience in generating delinquent involvement, it is no surprise to find supportive data. Hirschi (1969) and Hindelang (1973) both report greater delinquency with lower academic achievement, negative school-related attitudes, and less involvement in school activities. Many others have found similar associations (see Gibbons, 1976:135-8, or Schafer and Polk, 1967, for a summary; see also Polk, 1971; Frease, 1973; Kelly and Pink, 1973; Slocum and Stone, 1963; Elliott and Voss, 1974). There seems to be no doubt that school success and school attachment deserve a place in any serious delineation of the factors producing delinquency. They, too, must therefore be incorporated into the model that will be developed in Chapter 3.

Perceptions of the future

One of the most-researched topics in the sociology of delinquency is that of the occupational and educational aspirations and expectations of adolescents, a tribute to the dominant influence of Merton's early strain theory. Two general questions emerge as important: What are the effects of class on aspirations and expectations? What are the effects of aspirations and expectations on delinquent behavior? The data present an ambiguous picture.

Some studies support the Mertonian proposal that basic cultural goals or aspirations are universal throughout the social structure. Jessor et al. (1968) find similar desires espoused by members of different ethnic groups. Elliott's (1961, 1962) data add support to the notion of broad acceptance of middle-class objectives and values, as do the data reported recently by Berman and Haug (1975).

On the other hand, Caro and Pihlblad (1965) and Berger and Simon (1974) report differences in the aspirations of lower-class and middle-class adolescents. And on the basis of a sample of rural Americans, Rushing (1970: 392) concludes that Merton's asserted goal of monetary success "appears not to be firmly entrenched toward the bottom of the class structure." Finally, Uzell (1961) reports no occupational–aspiration differences by SES measured by father's occupation, but he finds that there are significant differences measured by level of parent's education.

There are two principal difficulties in evaluating these data. First, are the studies sampling the theoretically relevant underclass, or are they simply studying blue-collar and white-collar earners? Perhaps in the core slum areas or among the truly destitute, the American dream does not apply. Clark and Wenninger's (1963) mixed findings shed light on this issue. They conclude that "major goal orientations are rather similar in nature throughout society" (p. 49) and find no goal differences between youths of different status families within communities. However, they also find that "significant differences in their [goals'] distribution are found in various communities" (p. 49). Thus a large concentration of underclass residents may be a prerequisite for the development of unique goal orientations. The sad fact is that "*systematic* data on the goals and aspirations of persons at the bottom of the class structure – persons at the poverty level – are virtually nonexistent" (Rushing, 1970: 378).

The second difficulty in making sense of these data is the nagging problem of validity of responses. Even presuming that lower-class or underclass adolescents verbalize lower occupational or educational desires, do they really mean what they say? Do they really want less because of differential socialization, or have their lower realistic expectations already forced a face-saving, defensive reduction in reported dreams or wishes?

In the first place, the expectations (realistically perceived opportunities) of lower-class respondents are definitely less than those of middle-class respondents (Elliott, 1961, 1962; Gold, 1963; Jessor et al., 1968; Kerckhoff and Huff, 1974). Furthermore, Rodman's (1963) theory of "value stretch" suggests that lower-class individuals share the middle class's high level of aspiration but proceed to stretch their "aspiration range" downward in view of scarce resources. He therefore predicts a wider range of lower-class aspirations, with an upper limit the same as the middle-class range, but a willingness to "want" or accept as "good" a lower bottom limit.

Rodman et al. (1974) have tested the value-stretch hypothesis, and the data support it for white males. This support adds weight to the argument of Caro and Pihlblad (1965) that their discovery of lower occupational aspirations among lower-class youth is caused by perceptions of limited access rather than differential evaluations of occupations.

The best conclusion seems to be that uncompromised aspirations (real wants) are highly similar across class lines, but that expectations are significantly lower at the bottom of the social scale. It seems that a Walter Miller-type dichotomy in these kinds of (futuristic) values does not exist; or, if it does, it is relegated to a small segment of society in homogeneous pockets of underclass individuals. It also follows that a Mertonian strain or discrepancy between goals and perceived opportunities is more prevalent among the lower class.

However, some studies fail to find a greater "aspiration minus expectation" discrepancy in the lower class (Berger and Simon, 1974; Bergman and Haug, 1975), but the range of social status reported in these studies is very limited. By contrast, Caro and Pihlblad (1965) and Empey (1956) report greater discrepancies among lower-SES respondents. And finally, no studies find greater aspirations or greater expectations within the lower class.

As discussed above, traditional strain formulations were developed to explain specifically *lower*-class delinquency. And, as just reviewed, there is evidence that perceived-opportunities strain is moderately related to socioeconomic background. Moreover, it is quite possible that there may actually be more delinquent behavior in the underclass of society. But overall, the evidence for the presence of substantial class-induced futuristic strain, or even for more immediate "status deprivation" (Reiss and Rhodes, 1963), is far from compelling.

In general theory building, an equally crucial connection is the linkage between strain and delinquency on the individual level, which does not require any particular class–strain association in order to exist in its own right. Traditional strain theories imply too great a pressure on selected individuals to deviate from self-accepted norms; that is, too great a commitment either to deviance or to conformity. They do not adequately account for the sporadic, episodic, and pervasive nature of self-reported delinquent behavior. But a recognition that perceptions of future opportunities and barriers can generate delinquency in all social sectors is a genuine contribution of strain formulations. As Elliott (1962:227) concludes, "Thus middle-class delinquency may be a response to the same general problem of adjustment as is lower-class delinquency."

Elliott bases this conclusion on data showing that official delinquents in both the middle and the lower classes perceive fewer future success opportunities than do nondelinquents. Research apparently supports the separate conclusions that (*a*) greater delinquency is associated with lower educational-occupational aspirations (Elliott, 1961:114; Clark and Wenninger, 1963; Hirschi, 1969; Hindelang, 1973; Short, 1964; Gold, 1963; Spergel, 1961), (*b*) greater delinquency is associated with lower educational–occupational expectations or perceived opportunities (Short et al., 1965; Clark and Wenninger, 1963; Datesman et al., 1975; Gold, 1963:14; Elliott, 1961; Fredericks and Monar, 1969), and (*c*) greater delinquency is associated with larger discrepancies between educational–occupational aspirations and expectations (Elliott, 1961; Short, 1964:105–15; Spergel, 1961; Short and Strodtbeck, 1965:269; Quicker, 1974).

The conclusions that aspirations and expectations are each independently related to delinquency are, of course, consistent with control theory. They represent commitments to conventional lines of activity, which give the individual a stake in conformity. The third conclusion – that the discrepancy itself is delinquency generating – supports a strain rather than control formulation. And it is this third conclusion that is on shakiest grounds.

In the first place, all but one (Quicker, 1974) of the supportive studies cited employ official measures of delinquency. Being a known and labeled offender is quite likely to produce a feedback effect of expectations lowered from aspirations. Every juvenile knows that having a record may count against him or her in future educational or employment pursuits. So the strain or discrepancy is just as likely an effect as a cause of official delinquency. Secondly, the author reporting an effect of discrepancy on self-reported behavior downplays the magnitude of the relationship: "Planning far ahead, worrying about the very distant future, is, in this rapidly changing world, just not a powerful cause of much frustration" (Quicker, 1974:85).

Furthermore, several careful analyses suggest either that aspiration–expectation discrepancies are unrelated to self-reported delinquency (Voss, 1966; Schoenberg, 1975:70; Hirschi, 1969:173) or that their apparent effects are in fact "accounted for in terms of the additive formulation as a simple inverse function of educational and occupational expectations" (Liska, 1971:105). Thus it seems that expectations alone may be clearer indicators of strain (i.e., perceptions of future chances for success or failure) than are the more complicated discrepancy scores.

One reason for discontinuing the use of discrepancy scores is that the validity of aspiration responses remains questionable, because of artificial lowering of true desires in order to cope with real circumstances and to maintain self-esteem. Most adolescents agree on the relative desirability of occupations (Gold, 1963:167; Elliott, 1961:114). It is not clear that reported variations in occupational desires are more than indirect measures of more realistically perceived opportunities. This problem complicates the interpretation of discrepancy measures as well as that of aspiration scores alone.

The upshot is that expectations are probably the most valid and theoretically consistent indicator of both strain and social bonds. Perceiving a real chance for career success certainly provides a greater stake in conformity, whereas expecting failure induces frustration. Commitment to conventional lines of activity and perceived opportunities are two sides of the same coin. Thus the proposals of both strain and control orientations are consistent with the data on the role of perceptions of the future in generating delinquency, and futuristic strain will be included in the model for testing.

Delinquent associates

In its broadest terms the subculture perspective states simply that deviance is committed in accord with deviant values and attitudes. These values and attitudes must come from somewhere, which means delinquent associates. From strict class-related versions like Walter Miller's to broad class-free formulations like Edwin Sutherland's, the subculture prediction is that delinquent associates are a tremendous influence in generating delinquent involvement. What do the data show?

It seems clear that self-reported delinquent behavior and delinquent associates go hand in hand (Hirschi, 1969; Hindelang, 1973; Liska, 1973; Erickson and Empey, 1965; Schoenberg, 1975; Linden and Hackler, 1973; Conger, 1976). And, in fact, the majority of delinquent acts seem to be committed in the company of other juveniles (Erickson, 1973; Reiss and Rhodes, 1961; Carter, 1968). The role of peer influence in generating delinquency is not so clear, however.

Does a general peer orientation or peer attachment produce or control delinquency, or does it depend on the type of peers with whom the adolescent associates? Erickson and Empey (1965) report a positive association between theft and general commitment to peers. Similarly, Polk (1971) cites peer orientation as a correlate of admitted delinquency. By contrast, Conger (1976) reports no relationship between attachment to peers and self-reported delinquency in a sample of seventh graders. Hirschi (1969) concludes that peer attachment acts to control delinquency and is itself positively related to parental attachment, although Hindelang's (1973) data fail to duplicate those results. It seems safe to hypothesize that the degree of delinquent involvement of friends conditions the nature of peer influence on delinquent behavior, as reported by Linden and Hackler (1973).

Tangentially, the stereotype of unusually binding ties among more delinquent peers – "blood brothers in crime" – does not receive support in the literature. There is no evidence that sharing deviant experiences results in any closer ties among friends than does sharing conventional experiences. Neither does "deviating together" seem to require fast friendship. Haney and Gold (1973) report delinquency as occurring in the company of a shifting number of friends. Empey (1967) depicts delinquents' interpersonal relations as highly defensive and stylized rather than supportive. Hewitt (1970:76) observes that "difficulties in getting along with other people" characterize "nearly all (habitual) delinquents." And finally, Hirschi concludes that the data are clear that:

> the interpersonal relations among delinquents are not of the same quality of warmth and intensity as those among nondelinquents; failure in one group decreases the likelihood that one will find intimate personal relations in some other group;

delinquents do not possess the skills requisite to the argument that they are somehow the finest products of their own culture [1969:229].

Regardless of the nature or quality of relationships among juvenile law violators, it is clear that the role of delinquent associates cannot be ignored when one considers the development of causal models of delinquent behavior.

Delinquent values

The question of personal commitment to delinquency norms, attitudes, and values follows naturally from the discussion of delinquent associates. The statement by Hirschi just quoted, for example, is made in part to deny the ability of delinquent juveniles to develop unique cohesive "subcultures of deviance."

Subculture theory, as noted earlier, is basically a proposition that delinquency results from conformity to a separate set of accepted norms and values. As such, it has not been refuted or even tested by data on the SES distribution of delinquency. Employing an underclass/earning-class model (UC/EC), the strict subcultural prediction would be that the underclass holds values more compatible with delinquency and therefore exhibits more delinquency. Little existing evidence bears on this question. Although the possibility of localized subcultures or contracultures in the underclass is granted, it seems doubtful that there is any great commitment to delinquency even there.

One reason for doubting very extensive personal commitment to delinquent values is the aforementioned sporadic nature of delinquency, with the eventual conformity of most young people who self-report delinquent acts. Additionally, Elliott (1961:79) reports uniform perceptions of behavioral norms and uniform attachments to social norms across SES categories. Jessor et al. (1969:34–7) cite "much available evidence of society-wide sharing of a variety of values relative to conformity" and are "unwilling to accept" the view that the norms of the lower (under) class directly support deviance. Maccoby et al. (1958:49–50) find that the residents of a high-delinquency area share the values of larger society about the wrongness and seriousness of juvenile stealing, property damage, and drunkenness. Glaser et al. conclude that their study "contradicts the image of uniformly enculturating high delinquency neighborhoods" (1971:510).

From these studies it appears that conduct values are approximately uniform across the social classes and may therefore lose importance in this context. But, on the subcultural side, there have been indications that homogeneous areas often exhibit the most delinquency (Reiss and Rhodes, 1961; Clark and Wenninger, 1962; Voss, 1966). Thus the model must remain incomplete. It is probable that the underclass also favors conventional values, but there may indeed be more commitment to delinquent norms, a lack of conduct norms, or simply greater tolerance of delinquent behavior at play in that social sector.

Yet these facts do not preclude the possibility of delinquent acts being committed in association with an individual's norms and values. In fact, it seems necessary to recognize that the practical norms and values of everyday life allow for situational deviation from ideals. Indeed, much of Sutherland's (1949) and Sutherland and Cressey's (1974) work directs its attention to the pervasiveness of definitions conducive to law violation throughout the class structure. Empey's (1967) "infraculture" and Matza and Sykes's (1961) "subterranean values" are restatements of the existence of these often very pragmatic, situationally deviance-condoning norms and values in American society. Looking ahead to the task of building and testing a general causal model, the most applicable contribution of the subcultural perspective is entailed in these related concepts.

Briefly, Empey's (1967) infraculture ("a ubiquitous, but amorphous, subculture") is the traditional acceptance in America of deviance as having symbiotic relationships with politics, economic growth, social change, and the like. America's brawling, individualistic tradition allows for nonconformity for the sake of principle, the greater good, or mere practicality. Situational departure from verbal ideals is not necessarily condemned but is recognized as relatively common and sometimes desirable or necessary. Schrag observes that "in complex societies nearly everyone recognizes certain discrepancies in the group's standards. This means that the individual, in order to conform, must exhibit in his own behavior the discrepancies found in his society" (1971:108). There is seldom congruence among norms, values, goals, and practices; "normative support for deviant behavior can readily be found in conventional society" (Schrag, 1919:110).

Matza and Sykes's (1961) conception of subterranean values applies more specifically to adolescents. Being in social limbo between childhood and adult status, and constituting a form of "leisure class," adolescents throughout society are especially vulnerable to values and norms favoring adventure, thrills, kicks, conspicuous consumption, easy jobs, and (for boys) proof of masculinity. Kvaraceus and Miller (1959: 77–9) concede that there is a society-wide concern with "toughness," and they imply antiestablishment feelings to youth in all social classes. Such feelings may be fostered by compulsory education or by compulsory conformity to the norms of dependency.

Research findings support the conception of an infraculture of situational acceptance of misbehavior in all social sectors. The view of a monolithic conventional set of middle-class conduct norms is no more reasonable than the position that lower-class youths are exposed exclusively to antilegal values. Kobrin's (1951) "conflict of values" or "duality of conduct norms" undoubtedly applies to some extent in all social sectors. It is clear that very respectable, well-to-do businessmen often act as models of manipulative behavior to their children (Epstein, 1967). And Weis (1973:24) cites further research showing substantial value variation within the lower class and within the middle class.

Of course, nearly all adolescents readily admit committing delinquent acts. Indeed, there is even concern with overreporting. There seems to be a common perception among adolescents that delinquent behavior is situationally expected and/or approved by their associates (Matza, 1964; Linden, 1974). Furthermore, Hindelang (1970) has found the values of middle-class youths to be inconsistent both internally and with traditional ideals. Alcohol consumption and sexual promiscuity are neither highly valued nor rejected, whereas fistfighting appears to be a generally accepted activity. The conclusion here is that delinquent acts may frequently be viewed as consonant with norms and values shared by many young people in all social sectors. It remains to be determined whether this infraculture is more profound or visible in the underclass.

The most reasonable stance seems to be one proposing individual degrees of acceptance of illegalities, but with very little hard-core commitment to delinquent prescriptions. Moreover, research should reveal an association between an adolescent's degree of acceptance of delinquent values and his or her extent of participation in illegal activities. Available data support both positions. Even highly involved delinquents tend to place higher value on conventional accomplishments than on success in delinquency (Short, 1964; Short and Strodtbeck, 1965; Short et al., 1965; Lerman, 1968). And degree of belief in the validity of conventional conduct norms does in fact correlate with delinquent involvement (Hirschi, 1969; Hindelang, 1973, 1974; Hepburn, 1976; Silberman, 1976) and with official delinquent status (Siegal et al., 1973; Elliott, 1961:104; Hepburn, 1976).

The task of sorting out the nature of the interrelationships among delinquent values, delinquent associates, and delinquent behavior is reserved for Chapter 3. Here it is sufficient to note that delinquent values have been shown to remain a tenable variable in the etiology of delinquency and will be included in this study for further testing. This is in sharp contrast to the position of those who, on the basis of self-report studies' apparent refutation of class theories, blindly throw the baby out with the bath and discard key variables simply because they have been incorporated in class-related formulations.

Deterrence

If fear of threatened punishment does in fact deter adolescents from illegalities they might otherwise commit, then the major theoretical orientations have neglected an important variable. Tittle and Rowe (1974: 461) claim that most delinquency theories overemphasize "push," or motivation to deviate, and add: "Were we to incorporate the notion of deterrence, we might move toward closure in our current theories. The most telling criticism of theories of deviant behavior is that they cannot account for negative cases . . . Perhaps the missing link is fear of sanction."

Of course, control theory is less vulnerable than strain or subculture views to this criticism, but it, too, has tended to ignore the possible delinquency-reducing effects of threatened official apprehension. Because of its relatively isolated development, the concept of deterrence should perhaps be briefly reviewed before the relevant data are examined (see Johnson, 1974, for a more complete discussion).

Deterrence came into its own as a primary rationale for legal punishment as part of classical criminology in the late eighteenth and early nineteenth centuries. Rationality, free choice, and similarity among all people were cornerstones of the thinking of the early deterrence theorists like Cesar Beccaria (1764) and Jeremy Bentham (1830). After giving way to so-called positive criminology for many years, these classical presumptions are once again receiving scholarly attention and theoretical emphasis (cf. Matza, 1964; Gibbs, 1975).

Bentham's doctrine of the "calculus of pleasure and pain" depicts man as rationally calculating the positive and negative consequences of any act before committing (or being deterred from) the projected act. Consequently, if punishment is foreseen as a *certain* consequence of delinquency, the potential delinquent will be deterred if the punishment is judged even barely more painful than the degree of pleasure (relief from strain, impressing peers, economic reward, etc.) to be gained. To quote Bentham: "In matters of importance every one calculates. Each individual calculates with more or less correctness, according to the degrees of his information, and the power of the motives which actuate him, but all calculate. It would be hard to say that a madman does not calculate" (1830:41). It is, of course, the potential delinquent's perceptions of the pleasures and pains rather than the objective rewards and punishments that determine the result. Deterrence is a psychological process and concept. To emphasize this point, Bentham differentiated between the "real punishment" (actual suffering inflicted on the body of the offender) and the "apparent punishment" in the minds of potential criminals. As he put it, "the real punishment ought to be small, and the apparent punishment as great as possible" (1830:29).

Throughout their writings, Bentham and Beccaria state and imply that the mechanism through which deterrence works is fear or intimidation. That is, the motivation to conform is based upon a negative orientation to negative consequences and not upon positive bonds to social institutions. Bentham recognized the latter forces but chose not to include them in his discussion of "determent" or "general prevention." He noted that the pleasure–pain calculus – if criminal pleasure wins out – will result in crime "by those who are only restrained by the laws, and not by any other tutelary motives, such as benevolence, religion, or honor" (1830:33 n).

Fear of threatened legal punishment, then, fits nicely into the general conception of a "stake in conformity"; that is, conformity in this case ensures the avoidance of negative societal reaction. But conceptual clarity requires that deterrence remain an analytically distinct construct. There is a qualitative difference between conforming in order to maintain rewarding relationships and opportunities and conforming in order to avoid a specific punishment. Of course, punishment can be broadened to subsume such consequences as guilt or attenuation of parental ties, but usage of a deterrence conception is best limited to the official punishments of the justice system (police apprehension, court appearances, institutionalization, etc.).

Furthermore, the mechanisms by which the existence of official punishment can prevent delinquency are more numerous than simply deterrence – conformity due to the fear of threatened punishment. The most extensive discussions of indirect mechanisms through which the threat of punishment may induce compliance with the law are found in Zimring and Hawkins (1973:77–89) and Gibbs (1975). Legal threats may prevent crime also by being teachers of right and wrong, mechanisms for building respect for law, habit builders, and rationales for conformity.

By way of brief elaboration, the constant association of a punishment with a given act may lead to the perception that the act itself is inherently wrong. Thus the threat of punishment for an act socializes the offender against the act, thereby influencing delinquent personal values. Threats may also initiate conforming behavior that later becomes habit. The threatened punishment may be forgotten or even removed, whereas the behavior continues. Finally, under many conditions adolescents feel pressures (from peers or unusual situational factors) to break a law, while still feeling wrong about doing so. In these cases the fact of the existence of threatened punishment may be called forth to provide an excuse or rationale for conformity.

Surely these are some plausible ways in which threats of punishment may reduce deviance. Perhaps it seems too technical to object to these as expansions of the deterrence process, yet there are valid reasons for retaining the more narrow construction of deterrence as distinct from other preventive effects of threatened punishments.

One reason for retaining the more classical conception of deterrence is that it involves the direct effects and conscious consideration of threatened penalties, as opposed to the four listed indirect and largely unconscious influences. Deterrence requires an awareness of a threat (it need not be accurate, however), whereas "general preventive effects do not occur only among those who have been informed about penal provisions and their applications" (Andenaes, 1966:951). Moreover, most of the indirect effects occur only after a great time lag and repeated exposure to specific threats, which further differentiates them from deterrence.

There is yet another qualitative distinction between deterrence and the so-called indirect effects. In balance notions or control theory, the indirect effects represent positive attachments or bonds to conforming aspects of society – respect for the law, acceptance of conformity as good, a habit of law-abidingness, and so on. By contrast, deterrence is conformity resulting from negative bonds (fear) to negative consequences (official sanctions). And it applies only in cases in which the positive bonds have failed to control deviant tendencies.

Control through deterrence seems to occupy a unique, last-resort position in a control formulation. The traditional positive bonds operate to insulate people differentially from temptations to commit illegal behavior. Most adolescents consequently do not need to weigh the consequences of sanction threats in order to conform to most laws most of the time. But for those likeliest to engage in illegality after the positive controls operate, a final negative control is applied - the threat of punishment. The result in any given case is deterrence or deviance. Of course, this is an idealized conceptualization, as in reality all controlling factors operate simultaneously in complex ways. The point is that deterrent control is a likely candidate for inclusion in a general control or bonding formulation.

In sum, deterrence is most fruitfully viewed as a conscious process resulting in conformity to laws. As such, it assumes awareness of the existence of an external threat of undesired consequences, whether it be a correct or incorrect perception. Its conceptual existence does not of necessity present the person as a mechanical calculator of pleasure and pain at every turn, as many critics maintain. It allows for other factors and processes in the causation or prevention of delinquency. Indeed, it is presented as a concept that applies only to situations in which an individual is faced with a real decision to conform or deviate. The assertion that deterrence occurs as a conceptually distinct phenomenon contains no assertion about its frequency of occurrence, which is undoubtedly exaggerated in classical theory yet extensive in human behavior.

The threat of a given punishment (*P*) is a deterrent for a given person (*A*) with respect to crime (*c*) at time (*t*) *if and only if* (*A*) does not commit crime (*c*) at time (*t*) *because* he believes he runs the risk of (*P*) if he commits (*c*) and he prefers, ceteris paribus, not to suffer (*P*) for committing (*c*). Deterrence implies that the deterred will not offend and that the offender is not deterred. However, as only one of several mechanisms through which threats may induce conformity - and with threats as only one of many factors influencing conformity - deterrence reasoning does not imply that the nonoffender is deterred, or that the nondeterred is an offender (cf. Bedau, 1970). Conformity can occur for reasons other than the psychological process of deterrence. And many who do not consider threatened punishment are conformists for other reasons. Finally, deterrence does not imply any personality or morality changes in the deterred individual.

The likelihood of deterrence occurring, of course, is in part determined by individual characteristics or by the nature of the offense (cf. Johnson, 1974; Zimring and Hawkins, 1973; Andenaes, 1975). Furthermore, both Bentham and Beccaria developed lists of factors that would condition the deterrent effectiveness of a threatened punishment. Beccaria noted that deterrence would increase if punishment were public, prompt, of long duration, and "analogous" to the crime (in nature and in severity). He further asserted that "The certainty of a punishment, even if it be moderate, will always make a stronger impression than the fear of another which is more terrible but combined with the hope of immunity" (1764:58).

Bentham's list of conditioning factors included the intensity (severity), proximity (celerity), certainty, and duration of the punishment as the "value of pain." He further added the punishment's "characteristicalness" (similarity in kind to the crime), "exemplarity" (ratio of apparent to real magnitude), and "simplicity of description" (so that the entire sanction is in the tempted's mind) as factors related to deterrent efficacy. Like Beccaria, he viewed certainty of punishment as the "first line of defense" in deterring crime, with the severity to be increased only to compensate for inadequate certainty or proximity.

In exploring the data, then, the focus will be upon results bearing on the relative importance of the certainty and severity of legal responses in curbing deviance. Celerity is often mentioned as a third crucial dimension of threats. The speed of past applications of punishment undoubtedly increases the salience of the threatened punishment in the audience's thinking. It seems to exert greatest influence, however, as one of the factors creating a crime–punishment cognitive link, and as such it contributes to the total "perceived certainty" of sanctioning.

A great number of relevant research findings have been reported and synthesized by Andenaes (1975), Zimring and Hawkins (1973), and Palmer (1977). Tittle and Logan (1973) present perhaps the best concise, yet comprehensive, review of available evidence for and against "deterrence theory" (the assertion that threatened punishment does prevent the prohibited behavior through the deterrence process). Their conclusion is as follows:

Almost all research since 1960 supports the view that negative sanctions are significant variables in the explanation of conformity and deviance . . . It is clear, however, that the evidence is not conclusive. At this point we can safely say only that sanctions apparently have some deterrent effect under some circumstances [Tittle and Logan, 1973:385].

The data, however can serve only as a very indirect test of a presumed relationship between delinquent behavior and perceptions of the risks and/or costs of official apprehension. First, almost all of the studies employ external or objective measures of certainty and severity and assume them to indicate subjective perceptions. Second, they generally entail only adult felony statistics.

Perceived certainty of punishment is the effect of several factors, only one of which is "true" certainty. Celerity of past dispositions was mentioned above as another factor, largely because of the vague and general impression it creates about the degree of law enforcement efficiency. Likewise, publicity given to key arrests, to new methods, or to new personnel in law enforcement is likely to influence perceived certainty. The visibility of police and patrol cars is yet another factor. Finally, personal experiences with getting caught or getting away with an illegal act - and hearing similar stories from friends - exert perhaps the greatest influence on perceptions of risk.

From the studies dealing directly with perceptions of risk, it seems that these factors operate to produce considerable misperception of the actual probability of apprehension and punishment, specifically an overestimation of legal efficiency (see Jensen, 1969; and British Government Social Survey, reported in Zimring and Hawkins, 1973:167). This is not surprising, because the objective certainty is so low, even using offenses known to police as a base. For Index crimes in the United States in 1965, for example, approximately sixteen of every seventeen known felonies resulted in no imposition of sentence (Schrag, 1971:3). The uncertainty factor is undoubtedly greater for minor offenses, and for *all* offenses considering also unreported crimes. And self-reported delinquency seems to enjoy an extremely high rate of official nondetection (cf. Williams and Gold, 1972; Murphy et al., 1946). As one would expect, those with greater criminal involvement are more realistic in their perceptions of the chances of punishment and report lesser expectation of being caught or brought to justice (British Government Social Survey, in Zimring and Hawkins, 1973:167; Jensen, 1969).

Similar factors operate in a comparison of perceived and objective severity. Objective severity itself is confused, as the laws on the books often give wide sentencing discretion to judges. Moreover, judges have ways of skirting prescribed penalties. However, the data here, too, indicate widespread public ignorance of prescribed penalties for various crimes (see Zimring, 1971:57). Again, those more criminally involved show more accurate knowledge of penalty severity (Miller et al., 1971). However, the public's ignorance of exact penalties does not mean that people lack a general idea of severity – especially relative severity.

Studies of perceptions of certainty and severity as deterrents have been rare until very recently. Some researchers of late have found a negative correlation between perceived certainty of punishment and self-reported deviance (Teevan, 1976*a* and 1976*b*; Silberman, 1976; Erickson et al., 1977; Waldo and Chiricos, 1972), whereas others have found no such correlation (Bailey and Lott, 1976). None of these cross-sectional studies finds an inverse relationship between deviance and perceptions of the severity of punishment. Of course, an inverse relation between perceived certainty and criminality leaves open the question of causal direction, which will be discussed later.

In related research, several crime-trend studies have focused on the deterrent effects of increasing severity of punishment. Rusche and Kirchheimer (1939:200) found "no basis for assuming that the policy of punishment affects criminality" after examining crude indexes of crime and punishment trends in England, France, Italy, and Germany from 1910 to 1928. Schwartz (1968) found rape rates in Philadelphia increasing continually despite increases in penalty severity. And finally, the Assembly Committee on Criminal Procedure in California (1968) found similar results with marijuana possession and assaults on police in Los Angeles. However, control groups were universally lacking, so that it is unknown how the crime rates would have changed if threatened penalties had been unchanged.

Certainty of punishment has fared better in time-series studies. However, these mostly deal with traffic offenses, and the reported crackdowns on violations have often included an increase in penalty severity as well as in probability of detection. Still, increases in sanction probability have been shown to have reducing effects on speeding, parking, and drunk-driving violations (Campbell and Ross, 1968; Chambliss, 1966; Zimring and Hawkins, 1973:169–70; see also Andenaes, 1966).

The most profuse development in deterrence research has been the recent utilization of national crime and prison data in cross-state comparisons, with states as units. Gibbs's (1968) original study dealt only with homicide and measured certainty as a ratio of a state's prison admissions for murder in 1960 over mean number of known murders in 1959 and 1960. Severity was measured by the median number of months served by a state's homicide inmates as of December 1960.

Both Gibbs (1968) and Gray and Martin (1969) – utilizing the same data but different statistics – find both certainty ($r = -.28$) and severity ($r = -.37$) to be significantly inversely related to homicide rates. Again using the same data, Bean and Cushing (1971) point out that whereas region alone explains 62 percent of the states' variance in murder rates, certainty and severity explain an additional 7 percent (they explain 22 percent without consideration of region). All of these authors conclude merely that the case against deterrence is not proven.

Tittle (1969) extends this type of analysis to all seven Index crimes, using very similar measures of certainty and severity. He reports "strong and consistent negative associations" (p. 409) between the certainty and crime rates measures (Tau *c*'s ranging from −.08 to −.57, with a combined −.45). Concerning severity and offense rates, all are positive except for homicide (−.45), contrary to deterrence theory.

Interestingly, Tittle notes that the deterrent effects of certainty are greater in areas of lowest urbanization, which may reflect the greater visibility and stigma of punishment in those areas. Also, certainty itself is greater in less-urbanized areas and, ironically, in areas of lower police-to-population ratios. This latter finding shows that increasing the number of police does not necessarily increase police efficiency, or perhaps that police-to-population ratios are higher in urban areas where detection is most difficult. Finally, the surprising positive relations between severity and offense rates for all but murder disappear when controlling for level of urbanization, and the strength and behavior of the certainty correlations vary widely. Tittle concludes that certainty of imprisonment does have a deterrent effect but that "optimal deterrence conditions may vary widely for different kinds of offenses" (p. 417).

Chiricos and Waldo (1970), Logan (1972), Antunes and Hunt (1973), Erickson and Gibbs (1976), and Bailey et al. (1974) have all conducted similar analyses with very similar measures. Without belaboring the point, suffice it to say that results are similar even though interpretations vary. Consistently, variable moderate negative relations (averaging about .4) are found between certainty of punishment and crime rates, whereas for severity a negative association is found only for homicide.

Additionally, Chiricos and Waldo find no pattern in the associations of changes in certainty and severity and changes in crime rates, and Logan and Antunes and Hunt find some evidence for an interaction effect of severity and certainty on crime rates. This latter finding is consistent with the fact that severity seems salient only for homicide, which is the only offense for which the certainty of imprisonment is of any reasonable magnitude. The tentative hypothesis is that it takes a particular degree of certainty to make severity salient to a potential offender, but the evidence is scant at best.

Three studies employing related methodology have produced particularly interesting results. Tittle and Rowe (1974) find negative correlations between crime rates and arrest-clearance rates (certainty) for all counties and municipalities in Florida. They report that "results clearly support a deterrent argument, although the effect was found to be contingent upon the probability of arrest reaching a certain minimum level (about 30 percent)." Bailey (1976) cautions that these findings mask important differences across specific offenses but does not challenge the general conclusion.

Finally, Ehrlich (1973) has conducted a very sophisticated analysis, once again using national FBI statistics (with data from 1940, 1950, and 1960). Certainty and severity are again measured almost exactly as by Gibbs (1968). Not only does he find widespread support for the deterrent effectiveness of greater certainty and severity, but he relates many other factors to the certainty measure. Some variables inversely related to certainty are population size, population density, and percentage of juveniles. Correlating positively with certainty are level of adult schooling, relative poverty, percentage nonwhite, and police expenditures.

Accepting the general pattern of these data, there remains the issue of their relevance to the bulk of adolescent illegal deeds. They do in fact add to the tenability to the proposition that those juveniles who perceive their chances of getting caught as *less,* are then *more* likely to engage in delinquency. Claster's (1967) data support this notion, as delinquents perceived their personal risk of apprehension to be less than did nondelinquents, even though both groups perceived similar risks of general apprehension. Of course, causal direction is equivocal, as being more delinquent and adept at escape could lead to perceptions of lower risk.

The relative magnitude of the effect of fear of punishment in the overall scheme of delinquency causation is also problematic. In a survey of fifteen- to twenty-one-year old males by the British government, most listed more traditional social bonds as the greatest controls against their criminal involvement. Specifically, two-thirds said that likely disapproval by significant others (family, girl friends) most effectively kept them from deviating. Only 10 percent cited the punishment itself as their greatest deterrent (summarized in Zimring and Hawkins, 1973: 192). But questions of magnitude and causal directions aside for now, there is empirical support for including deterrence conceptions in a general causal model of delinquency.

Summary

The data reviewed in this chapter were intended to demonstrate that several variables, asserted or implied by the major theoretical orientations to be related to delinquent behavior, are in fact so associated. Basically this review has simply substantiated (or failed to reject, because of methodological problems in some studies) a series of bivariate correlations – each probable cause correlated separately with delinquency. In other words, these variables seem to deserve some role in a causal theory.

The available evidence indicates that *social class,* if reconceptualized into an underclass/earning-class (UC/EC) model, may indeed influence delinquent tendencies. There seems to be no doubt that the nature of *parent–child ties* plays some causal role. Likewise, the delinquency-generating influences of *school* failure and dislike for school seem unquestionable. The importance of *future-oriented strain* is not so clear. Indications are that on an individual basis in all social strata, perceptions of future educational or occupational failures or blocked opportunities contribute to a tendency to deviate from conventional social norms. The effect on delinquency of a general peer orientation seems dependent upon the degree of delinquent involvement of friends. Association with more *delinquent peers* definitely predicts higher amounts of personal delinquency. The role of *values and norms* relative to conformity and deviance appears, as does the role of strain, to be less class-specific than is often implied. There is very little evidence for the existence of hard-core delinquent life styles. Yet within all segments of the class structure, those most accepting of law violations are also most guilty of illegalities. And finally, it seems that *perceptions of the risk of apprehension* for delinquent acts are inversely associated with the commission of those acts.

This listing of relevant variables is at best only a crude skeleton of a theoretical formulation. The purpose of the next chapter will be to weave these elements together into a logically consistent and empirically justifiable causal model of delinquent behavior, which will then be tested against new data.

3. Tying the pieces together: a causal model

The theoretical propositions and research findings reviewed in the first two chapters have centered on causes of delinquency. Not much has been said about exactly what is the dependent variable in each case and specifically to whom each analysis is meant to be applicable. Such vagueness is perhaps justifiable (and perhaps even necessary) in a general literature review. But in order to present a useful, testable model, the intended scope must be more precisely delimited.

The scope of the theory

The specifics entailed in the actual measurement of the theoretical constructs are covered in Chapter 4, but here the aim is to verbalize the sense of what it is the model will try to explain. At the outset, it should be restated that the focus is on "delinquent behavior" as a continuous variable rather than "delinquency" as an official status. The goal is to describe those processes that lead to the likelihood or degree of involvement in illegal acts by juveniles. In this view, the crucial questions can be exemplified by imagining a situation in which adolescent law violation is a real possibility; that is, the temptation is there. The crucial questions the model will address are as follows: (*a*) What forces determine the probability that a given juvenile will even be in such a situation? And (*b*) what factors influence the probability that deviance rather than conformity will be the situational outcome? Thus the formulation is grounded in the presumption that delinquent behavior causation is a probabilistic and situational phenomenon.

As specific measures will indicate, this study retains a very legalistic or criminalistic conception of the dependent variable. Lack of consensus about the proper measure of delinquency has been the source of extensive debate, muddled arguments, and contradictory results (cf. Gold and Voss, 1967). This is true even within the rubric of self-report methodology, which will be employed here. This study is based on the presumptions that delinquent behavior is measured better by self-report than by official statistics and that delinquent behavior is a clearer construct if restricted to acts that would be chargeable offenses for adults as well as adolescents. In other words, there will be no attempt at explaining trivial misbehavior, such as talking back to parents, or so-called status offenses, which are illegal only because the actor is underage (smoking, drinking, etc.). This is not to say that similar forces are not involved in producing those behaviors. Nor does this restriction imply a lack of association between status and criminal offenses. The conception of delinquent behavior is restricted primarily for the sake of conceptual clarity.

Within the realm of chargeable criminal acts, the use of a single causal model presumes that there is a commonality of causal mechanisms. That is, this effort will conceptually bring together types of acts that some may prefer to analyze separately. Arnold (1965), for example, claims that theft, vandalism, and assault are independent dimensions of adolescent deviance. Gold (1966) suggests that offenses committed alone may be the result of influences different from those motivating offenses committed in a group context. These are valid concerns, and some possible interactions in the data will be examined in Chapter 6. But the general intent here is to integrate portions of major orientations into a model of why adolescents do or do not break the law. And it is fair to say that, at this point, the different types or "dimensions" of delinquent behavior have not been shown to correlate in significantly different ways with relevant variables (see Arnold, 1965).

Likewise, the model is intended to apply to American males and females of all races and social classes throughout the adolescent age range. The observation that "considerable evidence indicates that delinquents do come in an assortment of patterns" (Gibbons, 1976:98) does not mean that *at this point* it is necessary to separate out "working-class," "female," and "behavior-problem" delinquencies as distinct types with separate causes. It is wiser first to check the plausibility and generality of the overall model. Then refinements and details that undoubtedly follow (presuming general support for the model) will be of much greater theoretical value.

Moreover, available data provide no compelling reason to deny the similarity in etiology of the great bulk of American delinquent behavior. Regarding race, Berger and Simon (1974) conclude that their data fail to support Moynihan's implications of great racial differences in family experiences or the delinquency-relevant outcomes of those experiences. With social class, the review in Chapter 2 indicates that the data fail to support older notions of great social class differences. More and more researchers are crying for explorations into similar causal processes throughout the social class structure. As Matza and Sykes stated back in 1961, "it seems worthwhile to pursue the idea that some forms of juvenile delinquency - and possibly the most frequent - have a common sociological basis regardless of the class level at which they appear" (p. 718). A few whose works support this contention include Elliott (1961:130), Bloch and Niederhoffer (1958:17), Bloch (1963:20), Landis et al. (1963:414–15), Miller (1970:34), Polk (1971), and Gold (1963:13). Finally, Schoenberg (1975:104) "uncovered no race or class effects that could be accounted for by postulating a first or second order interaction." Simply stated, the same causal laws seem to apply across race and class subcategories.

The same conclusion about sex is somewhat more equivocal. Schoenberg does find some gender interactions. He concludes that the process of becoming involved in delinquent behavior "may be somewhat different for girls than for boys" (p. 108). However, he adds that the same influences have the greatest effects for both sexes. Similarly, Hindelang (1971*a*) reports the same patterns of delinquent behavior in males and females. The simple fact is that females have been overlooked in most delinquent behavior studies. It is thought that the model to be developed in this chapter will fit the data relatively well for both sexes. The logic involved is not restricted to one gender. It also seems that current trends for sexual equality in America are making the experiences of young men and women more similar to some extent. And finally, it is worth noting that those factors that loom large in discussions of specifically female delinquency (e.g., family ties, parental rejection) will hold key places in the general formulation.

Perhaps it seems presumptuous to attempt to explain the bulk of American society's delinquent behavior across the lines of race, class, sex, and type of offense. For the sake of balance, it is necessary to draw attention to some of the limitations of this analysis. In the first place, the formulation will primarily be on a social–psychological level of abstraction, with appreciation for the influence of selected societal features, such as the class structure. Thus the discussion will be simplified to the exclusion of both more cultural and more reductionist arguments.

Also, the focus of this work is only upon current American society, and not upon cross-cultural comparisons. Moreover, the literature review in Chapter 2 attempted to support the proposition that very few pockets of unique, definite subcultures of deviance exist within this society. Modifications in the causal analysis would be required to deal with those isolated areas of the social structure that may indeed enculturate delinquent behavior into young people. But in spite of these qualifications, it is proposed that the model to be delineated herein is as widely applicable as any other formulation.

At the other extreme, biogenic and psychogenic variables are excluded from the causal structure, partly for parsimony; but the exclusion seems empirically justifiable as well. To requote Gibbons (1976:73), "The many years of biogenic exploration of delinquency have not produced any valid generalizations about biological factors in deviance." He adds (p. 192), "The psychiatrist's claim that most delinquents are motivated by aberrant urges is unequivocally erroneous." However, there are undoubtedly some adolescents whose delinquent behavior is at least in part caused by genetic or biochemical difficulties and/or severe emotional disturbances (a fact Gibbons also recognizes, 1976: 192). These youthful offenders are simply exceptions to the rule concerning this theorizing and research. The important point is that they are also exceptions to the rule concerning the pervasive, situational, and episodic nature of the great proportion of delinquent behavior.

Even within the category of social–psychological variables, some must necessarily be excluded. Obviously, this study will not discover all of the causes of delinquent behavior. As Gold (1963:1) observes, "it seems inconceivable that all instances will someday be found to spring from one single factor or even one small set of factors" (cf. Friday and Hage, 1976:348). To be sure, the set of variables under consideration here represents a great simplification of a massive (and untestable) causal model that I developed previously (Johnson, 1973).

Most conspicuously absent from the scope of this discussion will be the supposed delinquent behavior-producing effects of official labeling as delinquent. The present study deals with the etiology of the extent of an individual's early delinquent involvement ("primary deviation," in the terminology of labeling theorists) rather than with causes of delinquency associated with a person's acceptance of a "permanent" deviant identity and deviant role career. Official delinquency status, with its attendant stigma and altered opportunities, certainly has some influence on the extent of future delinquent behavior. In fact, some of the possible feedbacks of official delinquency, as well as the extendability of general findings to a "labeled" subpopulation, will be examined in Chapter 6. But relatively few of those who commit delinquent acts are ever officially labeled (cf. Williams and Gold, 1972; President's Commission on Law Enforcement and Administration of Justice, 1967; Gibbons, 1976), so that the theory's general applicability is not seriously damaged. Furthermore, it would be unwise to exclude those who happen to have been apprehended from this study of causation of delinquent behavior, for causal studies must deal with as wide a range of the caused phenomenon as possible. Moreover, it is by no means clear that official societal reaction is an important unique influence in generating further misbehavior (Fisher and Erickson, 1973). It may prevent as much delinquency as it induces (Tittle, 1975).

In sum, the purpose of this chapter is to formulate an explanation of a wide variety of law violations committed by a wide variety of juveniles, focusing on social and especially social–psychological processes. Specifically excluded are those adolescents - only a very small minority - beyond a very broad range of "normal" intelligence, emotional development, and socialization, as probably requiring significantly modified delineations of causal processes.

Given the stated intention of analyzing middle-class as well as lower-class delinquent behavior, it should be noted that several formulations specifically directed at the middle class can be found in the literature. The major orientations discussed previously - strain, subculture, and control theories - either have been focused on the lower class or are class-free. And they do, in fact, make up the mainstream of sociological attention to the problem of delinquent behavior. As Weis (1973:vii) states, "Inquiry into middle class delinquency can be characterized as a theoretical wasteland and as an unproductive but uncultivated area of empirical research."

For the same reasons that theories exclusively directed at lower-class adolescents have been challenged (see Chapter 2), theories centered only on middle-class illegalities are of questionable value. Furthermore, theories of middle-class delinquency are neither very impressive logically nor supported empirically. Summaries are available in Vaz (1967) and Weis (1973), with the latter offering incisive criticisms. In short, notions such as masculine sex-role anxiety (Parsons, 1947; Cohen, 1955: 157–69), false embourgeoisement or "marginality" between social classes (Bohlke, 1961), decline of deferred gratification (Cohen, 1955), and diffusion of cultural values (Kvaraceus and Miller, 1959: 77–84) do not appear to be very helpful in developing a general orientation such as is proposed here.

However, several observations that were developed in reference to the middle class, but that apply to virtually all adolescents, will undoubtedly find their way into a general formulation. Indeed, Gibbons (1976:162–4) describes "lack of commitment" and "subterranean values" as "other theories of middle-class delinquency." But these are not concepts relevant only to middle-class delinquency; the relatively class-free nature of these social control conceptions has been discussed in earlier chapters. Likewise, a recognition of the ambiguity of the role of the adolescent in American society and of the widespread acceptance of hedonism among young people (England, 1960) can lead to insights into the behavior of youth in all social sectors. Empey (1967) also points out the general theme in theories of middle-class delinquency of identity difficulties and frustrations attendant on the transition from childhood to adulthood. There is no reason to presume that lower-class youth are somehow immune to these same influences. In short, many conceptions viewed by some as relevant only to the middle class are in fact more widely applicable.

On the basis of the available data, and in view of many theoretical claims, a "structural-equations" (path-analytic) model of self-reported delinquent behavior will now be developed. Many assertions of causal influence will be contained in the model, based upon Hirschi and Selvin's (1966) observation that the minimum criteria for an adequate demonstration of causality include (*a*) an observed association between the independent and dependent variables, (*b*) an ordering of the independent variable as causally prior, and (*c*) a remaining association when other variables causally prior to both are controlled, that is, nonspuriousness.

Although it is fairly simple to demonstrate correlations among the many pairs of variables in a causal scheme, the demonstrations of causal direction and nonspuriousness are often extremely problematic. Some assertions of causal direction will be soundly based on past research or the natural ordering of events, but others must rest on speculation. And nonspuriousness technically can never be proven, as there may always lurk some unconsidered prior cause of a given relationship.

The aim here is to include most of the possible prior causes that could lead to spurious associations in the model. There is no empirical opportunity to test the comprehensiveness of the list of variables in the model, so it must simply be assumed on theoretical grounds. It seems reasonably sure, however, that each of the two-variable subsystems is causally closed to unknown outside influence with respect to the covariation present.

And though there is always the possibility (indeed, probability) of feedback in causal direction in several two-variable subsystems, it seems that the field has progressed far enough to begin placing the key variables in at least an approximate weak causal ordering - a required assumption for a path analysis (Kim and Kohout, 1975). The claim is necessarily (and quite confidently) made that the ordering in the model occurs more often and with greater effect than the possible feedback alternatives. It is also possible to minimize the confounding of the causal ordering through carefully designed measures. But ultimately - with cross-sectional data such as are available in both the literature and in this study - it is impossible to test the propriety of the assumed causal ordering.

Path analysis of a "structural-equations" model is not a method for proving causality. Rather, it allows for "tracing out the implications of a set of causal assumptions which the researcher is willing to impose upon a system of relationships" (Kim and Kohout, 1975). The current body of delinquent behavior research is replete with often very atheoretical demonstrations of bivariate correlations. In many areas of inquiry the state of affairs can be characterized as stagnated and redundant. Even theory-guided studies such as Hirschi's (1969) leave much of the piecing together of the many relevant variables to the imagination. It is time to be willing to impose some assumptions on the causal structures and see what the data reveal about the plausibility of the thinking. In Gibbons's words (1976:88): "We need to discontinue the fact-gathering sorties that have been all too common, and turn to research which is designed to test explicit hypotheses concerning postulated relationships between particular psychological patterns, social influences, and delinquent behavior."

A causal model of delinquent behavior

It is difficult to label a theory of delinquent behavior that includes such diverse constructs as social class, perceived strain, attachments to parents and school, delinquent associates and values, and perceived risk of apprehension. The theoretically crucial constructs, however, seem to be

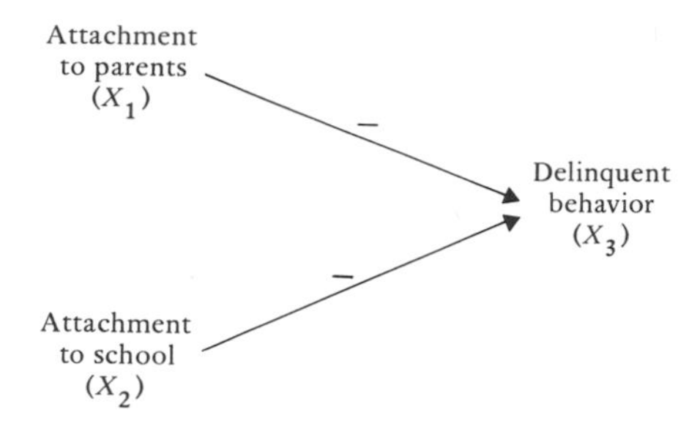

Figure 3.1. The basic attachment model

the attachments that an adolescent would form to his parents as well as to his school. These relationships, in fact, might make this an "attachment theory of delinquency." But this theory is actually much more.

The model building begins with the simple diagram given in Figure 3.1 (error terms and unanalyzed correlations are omitted for pictorial clarity). Delinquent behavior, of course, refers to the individual's degree of self-reported involvement in chargeable criminal offenses. Attachment to parents refers to the closeness of the parent–child relationship. It is basically an affective construct with a behavioral dimension. That is, it entails feelings of love, respect, desire to be near and to please parents; and it includes the actual sharing of time and feelings with them. The sign on the path from attachment to parents to delinquent behavior predicts an inverse relation – the greater the degree of parental attachment, the less the chance of situational involvement in law violation.[1] The unwritten presumption is the control theory reasoning that the "attached" youth thereby has a greater stake in conformity. Attachment implies a degree of mental presence of the parent in a situation in which the child is tempted to deviate; that is, "Will Mom or Dad find out? " and if they do, "How much does it matter to me? " The highly attached youth stands to weaken or even lose a rewarding relationship with a parent if caught in delinquent behavior, assuming that the parent prefers nondelinquent behavior on the part of the child. As Toby (1974: 87) puts it, the child who is unattached to the family "will have no great incentive to conform to the demands family members impose upon him."

It should be noted here that the effects of father and mother attachments are not presumed to be additive. It seems more reasonable to

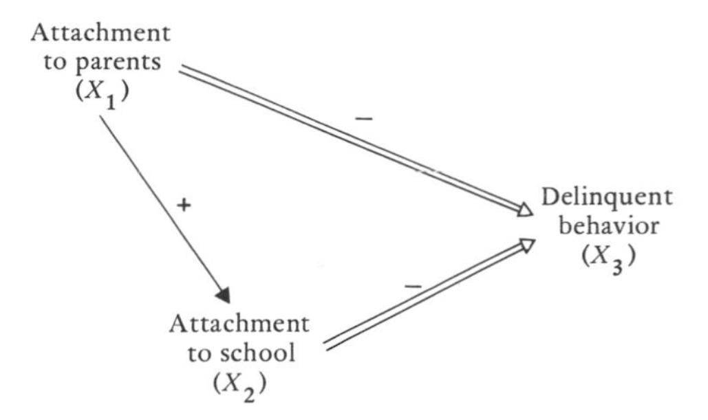

Figure 3.2. The sequential attachment model

postulate that a close tie to *either* father *or* mother is required to provide the delinquency-preventing stake in conformity.

Similarly, attachment to school entails enjoyment of school and school-related activities, positive feelings about teachers, and a willingness to put forth the effort necessary to succeed therein. It may be seen as containing the complementary dimensions of positive feelings about present school experiences and actual behavior aimed at present and future educational success. Such attachment, too, has been shown (as reviewed in Chapter 2) to be inversely related to delinquent involvement.

A final possible causal path in the three-variable model (Figure 3.2) is one proceeding from parent attachment to school attachment.[2]

Parental (father and/or mother) attachment has a great deal of time to form before the child even goes to school. And it does not simply begin first: It is easy to think of ways in which attachment to parents can consequently affect attachment to school. It is more difficult (but not impossible) to think of mechanisms that reverse the causal direction.

Assuming that a parent believes in the value of school success (at least valuing it over school failure), the child more attached to that parent can *please* the parent by doing well in school. That is, it is important for the parent-attached youth to fulfill parental expectations and hopes. The child will therefore be more likely to conform at school – at least behaviorally, via homework and so forth – to please the parents. This behavior pattern should occur independently of intelligence or actual past school success. At any level of success in school, those who have a greater parental bond also have more to lose by failing to attach themselves to school. Briar and Piliavin (1965:42) point out that the desire to achieve in school is often a product of parents' expectations that the child will perform well and the child's wish to fulfill those expectations (cf. McClelland et al., 1953; McKinley, 1964). In short, the child's attitudes and feelings toward one or both parents can influence his or her attitudes about (and consequently involvement in) conventional school experiences.

In related research, Watters and Stinnett (1971) and Clay (1976) both report "higher" occupational plans among children with closer ties to their parents. Such plans are indicative of greater commitment or attachment to the educational institution. However, the issue is complicated by Kerckhoff and Huff's (1974) finding "that the general quality of the parent–child relationship is unrelated to the degree to which the son adopts his parent's educational goals" (p. 323). Of course, similarity in educational goals is not the same variable as level of occupational plans, but there is enough complexity in these findings at least to indicate caution in asserting a direct link between parent and school attachments. Therefore, this effect is represented by a single rather than a double arrow in Figure 3.2.

Given that attachments to parents and school are key determinants of the likelihood of delinquent behavior, what determines the strength of those attachments? That is, what are the mechanisms of the bond formations? The model is expanded to include such mechanisms as indicated in Figure 3.3.

The invisible mechanism through which parental love and school success lead to attachments to parents and school, respectively, is the search for self-esteem. The theorizing here is strongly influenced by the work of John Hewitt (1970). Hewitt focuses upon the quest for self-esteem as the key to a child's formation of a bond (attachment) to society. This requires a priori assumptions of (*a*) a felt need for self-esteem in everyone and (*b*) a direct – although the causal effect may be in both directions – association between self-concept and behavior. To Hewitt, a deviance-preventing bond is formed whenever self-esteem is gained through relationships or experiences with conventional (or perceived as conventional) members of society.

First and foremost is the parent–child relationship. The amount of love or concern of the parent for the child should reflect itself in the ways the child feels he or she is treated by the parent. A child who is well treated by a parent feels good about himself or herself as a result of the experience: "They like me well enough to treat me with kindness, fairness, and respect. Therefore, I am worth something." People seem to invest themselves emotionally in those relationships from which they

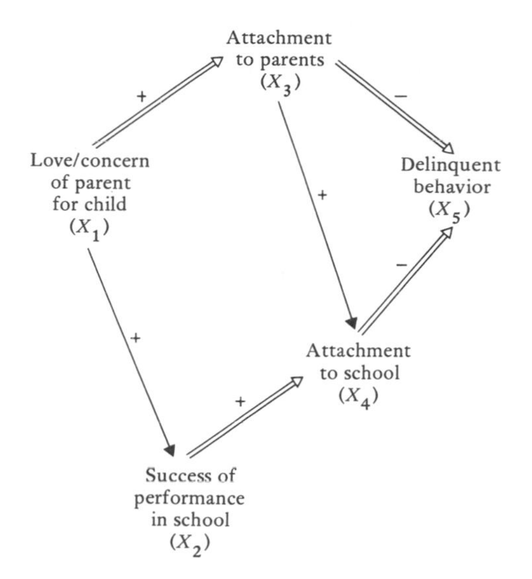

Figure 3.3. The model including determinants of attachments

derive such positive self-feelings. Hence, greater parental love – especially as it is perceived by the child – is a major cause of the child's attachment to that parent.

Nye (1958) has dealt with conceptions similar to "parental love for child" and "child's attachment to parent." He concludes that "acceptance–rejection by adolescent" is conceptually distinct from, yet correlated with (r = .42), "acceptance–rejection by parent." The present model would interpret inverse correlations between delinquent behavior and discipline techniques such as corporal punishment (cf. Gibbons, 1976: 132 ff.; Gold, 1963:14) and between delinquent behavior and parental rejection (Gibbons, 1976:132 ff.; Bandura and Walters, 1959:48–87) as operating at least partially through this process. Parental rejection and physical punishment fail to build self-esteem in (if not actively demean) the child, who is therefore less strongly attached to the parent. Hence, his or her stake in conformity is lowered.

Interestingly, McCord and McCord (1964) report that even when criminal conduct is modeled by the father, consistent love and discipline by the mother reduces misbehavior, whereas maternal rejection increases the child's criminal conduct. Thus only in those relatively rare instances in which *both* parents are in fact criminal does the theory seem to require the inclusion of a parental-deviance interactive effect.[3]

The school and public world (including clubs, organizations, etc.) also support and epitomize conventional norms and are seen by Hewitt as the next major influences in the development of self-esteem. At any point, the current attachment to school is in part dependent upon the amount of success the adolescent has enjoyed there in the past. The model proposes that a good deal of the empirical relationship between school success and delinquent behavior (see Chapter 2) is interpreted by the intervening effects of attachment to school. Poor school performance does appear to be related to dislike for school (Hirschi, 1969: 132; Polk, 1971; Downes, 1966).

The final path in the model so far completed (Figure 3.3) represents a direct influence of paternal love/concern for the child upon the child's chances for school success. It reduces to the proposition that, ceteris paribus, the more the parent cares for the child, the more he or she will aid and support the child in school, and thus the greater the child's success in school. In other words, children who are loved by mother and/or father should do better in school as a group than unloved children.

It is not true that mental ability predetermines school performance to the exclusion of parental influences, even though IQ apparently does affect delinquency through its effect on school performance (Hirschi and Hindelang, 1977). But in the etiology of delinquent behavior, it is school performance and not mental ability that seems to exert the greatest causal effects (Schoenberg, 1975:71). Short and Strodtbeck (1965: 236) speculate that gang delinquents come from those parents who have doomed their children to school failure by failing to provide them with adequate role-playing training. Perhaps some of this apparent parental neglect can be attributed to deficient abilities, but some might also arise from a lack of concern for the child's development.

Research results quite consistently support the proposition that school performance is influenced by parental love and concern. In a review of relevant studies, Watters and Stinnett (1971) state that "Consensus existed among the studies reviewed that academic achievement, leadership, and creative thinking of children was positively related to warm, accepting, understanding, and autonomy-granting parent-child relationships" (p. 91). They further report that parental acceptance is positively related to the child's IQ and that parental support is positively associated with the child's school achievement. Several more recent studies report similar findings (Mueller, 1974; Love and Kaswan, 1974; Hanson, 1975; Rehberg and Rosenthal, 1975).

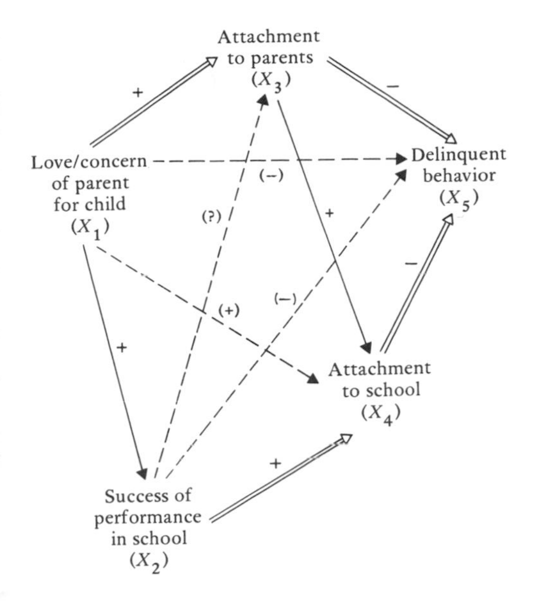

Figure 3.4. All possible effects in a portion of the causal model

Even confining the model to one-way causation (no feedback effects), there remain some unanalyzed logical possibilities for direct effects. Figure 3.4 shows these effects and represents the model thus far developed.

The previously omitted paths, represented here by dashed lines, are possible additions or alternatives to the formulation. Each arrow represents the direct effects of the first (independent) variable upon the second (dependent) variable, controlling for the effects on the dependent variable of all other causally prior variables. It is possible, for example, that success of performance in school has a direct causal influence upon delinquent behavior that is not mediated by attachment to school. Similarly, there is reason to believe that the love and concern of the parent for the child may directly influence attachment to school, irrespective of school performance (Kvaraceus and Ulrich, 1959; Robinson, 1975). All such possible routes are tested in a routine path analysis. But inclusion of all possible paths in a model quickly becomes very complex and virtually unreadable; so no further models will contain the dashed lines for possible effects. Every (X_i) is simply "vulnerable" to influence from every (X_j), with $j < i$.

Thus the diagrams summarize more than the proposed ordering of

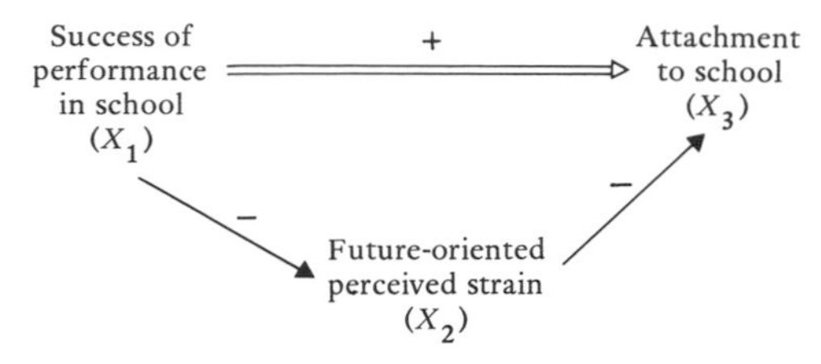

Figure 3.5. A model of the role of strain

variables and more than the asserted greater magnitude of effects of double arrows over those of single arrows. Assertions of the absence of direct effects are often extremely important theoretically, as will be seen with greater clarity later. For now, for example, the model logically implies that a parent's love for his or her child does not affect the child's conformity unless that love is translated into greater school success/attachment, or unless that love is reciprocated in the form of the adolescent's attachment to the parent.

The role of future-oriented perceived strain is added to an excerpt from the model in Figure 3.5. As discussed in Chapter 2, it is plausible that a Mertonian strain – the present perception of future educational and/or occupational failures (or limited opportunities) – may be involved in delinquent behavior causation throughout the class structure. If so, its place both logically and empirically is within the context of school experiences. Figure 3.5 proposes that strain plays a relatively minor role. It is presumed to be one mechanism through which school failure leads to detachment from school, but only one possible route.

A lack of school success is likely to generate anticipation of future educational and occupational difficulties (Gold, 1963:44; Caro and Pihlblad, 1965; Miller, 1970), although the effect is often rather minimal (Kerckhoff and Huff, 1974; Empey and Lubeck, 1971*b*; Clay, 1976). And anticipating occupational failure is somewhat predictive of delinquent behavior (see Chapter 2). The current proposal is that *if* strain affects delinquent behavior, it does so by causing a reduction in school attachment, which in turn affects delinquent behavior. That is, the natural result of giving up on the future is a similar giving up on the main road to that unattainable future – the present school experience (cf. Stinchcombe, 1964). The bond to school is attenuated both by past self-esteem-reducing school failures and by self-esteem-reducing percep-

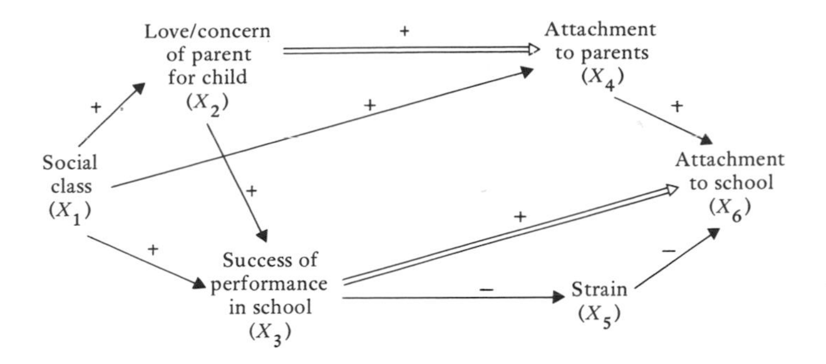

Figure 3.6. The model with social class and strain

tions of future failures. The model implies that the occupational future is less salient than the immediate past or present in generating frustrations and/or attachments, so that the direct path from school success to school attachment should overshadow the contribution of future-oriented perceived strain.

Social class is next added to part of the model in Figure 3.6, which represents the portion determining the crucial degrees of attachment to parents and school.[4]

The conception of social class employed in this theory is the underclass/earning-class model developed in Chapter 2. It is a dichotomous conception of the very poor versus the rest of society. Thus being from a very poor family (underclass) is presumed to affect negatively the child's chances for school success and for receiving rewarding, esteem-building treatment from his or her parents. Furthermore, social class (UC/EC) will not be presumed to relate to delinquent behavior in any way other than through generating differentials in parent and school attachments.

It is a common observation that lower-class children disproportionately lack success in school, even if class is measured by a series of SES categories. The effect should be exacerbated if class is more carefully measured in the UC/EC manner. As Hewitt (1970:60) observes:

> the propositions we have developed suggest class differentials in a number of obstacles (including school failure) to the pursuit of self-esteem but do not imply any necessary differentials in the *outcome* of self-esteem for members of different social classes, *except for those in the lower (under) class* [second emphasis added].

Jensen (1973) reports that adolescent self-esteem is positively associated with the level of the father's education and negatively related to "learning frustrations." Short and Strodtbeck (1965:236) assert that middle-class parents equip their children with "role-playing facility" adequate to succeed in school, whereas proportionately more lower-class parents do not. Gold (1963:14) joins those reporting greater school failure by lower-class children. Caro and Pihlblad (1965) find a high association between family SES and the academic aptitude of the student. Schafer and Polk (1967) add the weight of the data from the President's Commission on Law Enforcement and Administration of Justice to support the same conclusion.

Trotman (1977) reports a positive correlation between social class and several measures of school achievement for black and white ninth-grade girls. Hall et al. (1977) similarly find school achievement and IQ scores to be higher among middle-class students. Touliatos et al. (1977) report evidence of a direct relationship between socioeconomic status and scores on California Achievement Tests among black and white elementary school children. All of these data are consistent with the conclusion of Deutsch et al. (1967) that lower-class children suffer disabilities of almost every kind when it comes to effective participation in school.

Not every study finds social class a significant influence upon school success, however. Empey and Lubeck (1971*b*) and Rehberg and Rosenthal (1975) find little or no evidence of such a relationship. But these studies are in the minority and should not preclude the inclusion of this causal path in the model. Moreover, several studies have reported a relationship between class and strain (see Chapter 2, the section on perceptions of the future). The model asserts that this effect is mediated through school performance.

The model does not, and will not, detail the manner(s) through which being underclass decreases the likelihood of school success. Several plausible mechanisms have been suggested. One is the so-called middle-class bias of the American school system. In this view, typically middle-class teachers expect little accomplishment (and therefore find little, through a self-fulfilling prophecy) from the "poverty children." The evidence for this assertion is ambiguous. In a study of teachers' perceptions of photos of school children, the teachers did in fact expect better work from those viewed as coming from higher-SES families[5] (Harvey and Slatin, 1975). And teacher expectations have been found by some to influence school performance (Rosenthal, 1973; Rosenthal and Jacobson, 1968). These studies have been criticized and contradicted by others, however (Murphy, 1974). The best conclusion from reviews of the relevant studies is that the middle-class bias or Pygmalion effect is an extremely complex phenomenon. Whether it occurs seems to be determined by the interaction of several factors, and not just social class alone (cf. Braun, 1976; Wilkins, 1976).

Other ways in which class may affect school success include the possible placing of less emphasis on educational achievement by underclass parents. Kluckhohn and Strodtbeck (1973) suggest that lower-class parents care less about their children's school progress – an attitude the children are very likely to notice and accept. Similarly, Trotman (1977) finds an association between lower socioeconomic status and lower "home intellectual environment." The apparent result is a lower level of achievement motivation among underclass children (cf. Hewitt, 1970: 38–40). Finally, some writers have emphasized deficiencies in a lower-class environment that make school success problematic. These include poor language skills and a limited number and variety of opportunities for cognitive stimulation (Deutsch et al., 1967).

Underclass membership is similarly presumed to decrease the likelihood of a strong attachment to parents. The effect may be direct or be mediated through the parental-love construct. Taking the direct path first, the presumption is that the underclass parent simply fails to earn the respect of the child. It matters not how much the parent cares about the child, or even how much the child perceives that the parent cares – the child is simply less willing to attach himself or herself to a parent so obviously failing by society's success measures. As Gold (1963: 14) puts it, "attraction to the family (parent attachment) seems to depend to some extent on the social status of the family, lower status families having lower attraction potential." The same theme is repeated by Hewitt (1970: 144 ff.), Briar and Piliavin (1965: 41), and McKinley (1964: 92–3, 152–91). Mortimer (1976) points to the power of the father as a key variable in this discussion. He reasons that the socialization process is facilitated by a closer father–child attachment, which in turn is somewhat dependent upon the father's perceived power or ability to manipulate rewards that are meaningful to the child. One such reward is money. An underclass father, with little or no money, is thus less able to reward his child and thereby gain the child's allegiance or attachment. In a sense, attachment is "bought" to some degree in this view.

Being underclass is also likely to lessen the degree of real and/or apparent love and concern of the parent for the child. At the least, it can make it more difficult for the offspring to derive self-esteem from parental relationships. Given the fact that, by definition, underclass parents are plagued by immediate unemployment, poverty, and survival problems, one would not expect them to be as likely to enjoy the "luxury" of satisfying their children's needs for self-esteem. To do so takes time, presence in the home, and some degree of freedom from pressing psychological burdens - all of which may be problematic for the underclass parent (who is also more likely than the earning-class parent to be a single female head of household). Briar and Piliavin (1965) claim that lower-class children are more exposed to punishment, lack of love, and a general attitude of tension and aggression from early childhood (cf. Zegiob and Forehand, 1975). Corporal punishment seems especially unlikely to develop self-esteem (and hence to give the child a reason to invest himself or herself in the parental relationship). And corporal punishment appears to be more prevalent in the lower socioeconomic sectors (Kohn, 1969).

Following this reasoning, and following the analysis in Chapter 2 indicating the *possibility* of a real class (UC/EC) difference in delinquent behavior, social class is placed in the model. However, it would be surprising to find that its effects are large just because the construct has been reconceptualized. There are too many studies finding little or no association between SES and delinquent behavior to expect social class (UC/EC) to have great effect in delinquency causation. Indeed, a finding of no correlation between class and delinquent behavior would not damage the tenability of the more-central attachment propositions. Parental love would simply become an exogenous variable. The model merely offers a plausible interpretation of the manner in which class (UC/EC) affects delinquent behavior *if in fact it does.* Similarly, the fate of the general formulation does not depend upon a strong causal effect from class (UC/EC) to parent attachment. In fact, Berger and Simon's (1974) data question the existence of any such relationship. But theories are made to be tested, and social class will be included in those tests.

Hopefully, at this point in the theorizing process it is clear to the reader that the model is basically a social control orientation (see Chapter 1). Although expanded by the inclusion of class, strain, and self-esteem conceptions, the basic postulates so far are that (*a*) strong attachment to father and/or mother acts to prevent or control delinquent behavior and (*b*) strong attachment to school likewise prevents or controls delinquent behavior. So far there are no other postulated direct paths to delinquent behavior.[6] But this situation highlights perhaps the greatest predicament that social control perspectives experience – the absence of apparent motivation to commit illegal acts. If the lack of attachments frees an individual to deviate, what propels him or her from that circumstance beyond the brink of conformity?

From the literature review in Chapter 2, it is clear that no serious attempt at a general explanation of delinquent behavior can ignore the roles of delinquent associates and delinquent values. It is within these general headings that the motivation to deviate is likely to be found. There is no need to rely upon "animal impulses" or unusual drives to find provocation to deviate. The present conception of delinquent behavior as highly situational, along with a recognition of a pervasive infraculture of values conducive to situational deviance in American society, serves to fill the logical void. If delinquent values are viewed as a continuum along which the likelihood of accepting law violation under certain circumstances varies, there are few adolescents who have an absolute zero level of delinquent values. Almost everyone can imagine some situation in which he or she could accept delinquent behavior. The degree of delinquent values can be pictured as the range of such circumstances. In other words, adolescents are sometimes motivated into illegalities by seeing those acts as situationally acceptable. To quote Schrag (1971:96), "some criminal offenses . . . may be as much in accord with expressed values as are some legal conventions" in a complex society such as America. There is no need to postulate a monolithic, negativistic subculture of deviance (cf. Cohen, 1955) for delinquent values to play a role in generating delinquent behavior.

Given that situational acceptance of deviance is extensive, given that most adolescents associate with peers who exemplify these infracultural value systems, and given that a great deal of delinquent behavior is committed in the company of peers, it follows that peer associates also play a role in motivating delinquent behavior. Simply being in the company of others – each with a degree of situational acceptance of delinquent behavior in the name of such socially valued ends as excitement, loyalty to friends, daring, retributive justice, or possession of expensive goods – is likely sometimes to result in misbehavior. Thus the existence of delinquent associates is another variable that rarely reaches absolute zero, as it refers to the actual level of involvement in delinquent behavior of the

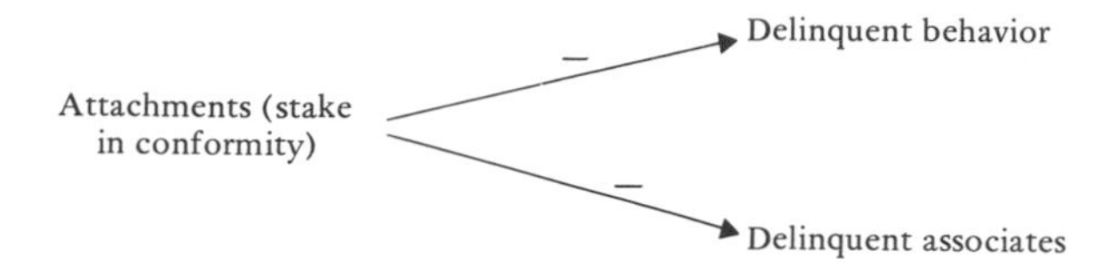

Figure 3.7. A strict control approach

adolescent's companions. Most of an adolescent's peers in a given situation have violated some law in the past, and this state of affairs can serve to provoke law violation by the uncontrolled adolescent.

Hirschi (1969:31–4) discusses these types of situational motivations (which parallel those discussed by Matza, 1964, and Briar and Piliavin, 1965), but largely dismisses them as excess baggage serving the function in control theory traditionally served by "animal impulses." It is unsatisfactory to answer the question of motivation by simply stating "we would if we dared" (Hirschi, 1969:34). Perhaps this attitude is what led Hirschi, by his own admission, to fail to appreciate the importance of peer associates as causal forces. It is more likely that delinquent associates and delinquent values – in ways similar to those described in the "differential association" (see Sutherland and Cressey, 1974) version of the general subculture orientation – have direct effects on the extent of delinquent involvement. The present model will therefore not hold to a strict control approach implying a solely spurious relationship between delinquent associates and delinquent behavior, as shown in Figure 3.7.[7]

Beginning with the attachment contructs, the model is expanded in Figure 3.8 to include a place for these additional variables. Figure 3.8 describes the central mechanisms through which attachments influence deviance or conformity. Viewed from a different angle, the model delineates a theory wherein the positive motivations to deviate are themselves reinforced by relative freedom from controlling bonds. Hirschi's assertion of the causal priority of parents and school over peers is, of course, retained. Hirschi feels that the stake in conformity the adolescent already has leads to his or her choice of friends, not vice versa. Hewitt agrees that the changing of significant others to reinforce established behavior patterns is more likely than the reverse. Essentially, it is a birds-of-a-feather-flock-together argument, and it makes sense. Those who are less attached to their parents, and *especially* those who are less attached to school (because of the higher visibility of school attach-

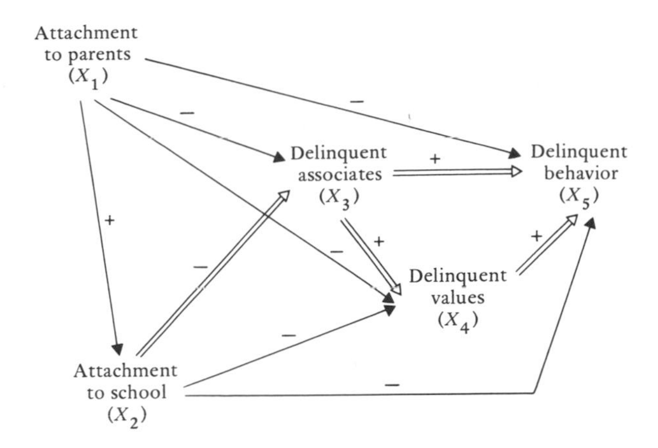

Figure 3.8. The model with delinquent associates and delinquent values

ment in the adolescent social world), will tend to find one another in the process of seeking and sorting companionships. As Briar and Piliavin (1965:40) claim, "stakes in conformity will influence the youth's choice of friends . . . Just as athletes, daters, and music lovers cluster together, so do those with similar commitments to conformity." Karacki and Toby (1962) present a similar argument.

Schoenberg's (1975) analysis of the data from three major self-report studies supports the tenability of Figure 3.8. He reports that "the variable affective ties (to parents) has a consistently moderate effect on delinquent association" (p. 82) and that "The appropriate general conclusion seems to be that school performance (and therefore school attachment) has a negative effect on delinquent association for all subsamples" (p. 82). He further finds that there are both direct effects on delinquent behavior of parent and school ties and (even greater) indirect effects through delinquent associations. In summation, Schoenberg (1975:85) states: "In any case it seems clear that both delinquent associations and the social control variables have effects on the seriousness of self-reported criminal offenses . . . thus differential association theory and social control theory seem to be supplementary rather than alternative theories."

As depicted in Figure 3.8, attachments may also affect delinquent behavior through altering personal value systems. That is, conventional parents and the school stand for antidelinquent values and directly socialize youth into the ways of conformity. The more attached the adolescent is to those institutions and people, the less willing he or she should be to define a particular law violation as acceptable. This formulation, of course, places higher priority in determining values on the social–psychological mechanisms of attachments than on more "structural effects" such as social class or area of residence. The direct path from underclass to delinquent values, for example, is not expected to be significant. The assumption is that parents and schools socialize against delinquent values there, too.

However, the explanation of the apparently unique phenomenon of seemingly hard-core gang delinquency in homogeneous lower-class neighborhoods may be problematic for this theory. Yet it seems plausible that even though small pockets of subcultural deviance may exist, there would still remain the inverse relationships between parental and school attachments and delinquent behavior. Indeed, it may be that among gang members in high-delinquency areas, low school attachment and low parental attachment approach the status of being subcultural norms, derived from extensive and generalized unsatisfactory relationships with parents and schools. At any rate, the theory does not require an active commitment to illegal conduct norms for values to exert a causal influence. All that is required is a degree of situational acceptance of law violation in the pursuit of socially valued ends, a degree of acceptance that is in part the result of the strength of ties to parents and school.

Attachments, then, affect delinquent behavior directly and affect the likelihood of having delinquent associates and of holding delinquent values. But how do these latter factors relate to one another and to delinquent behavior? As shown in Figure 3.9, delinquent values are postulated to have a direct causal effect on the individual's likelihood or extent of delinquent involvement. There is much evidence of an association between the two variables, as reviewed in Chapter 2 (see, for example, Ageton and Elliott, 1974; Liska, 1973; Siegal et al., 1973), even when the number of delinquent friends is controlled (Jensen, 1972 and 1973). As Hindelang (1974:383) says: "The data show quite unequivocally, for a wide variety of acts as well as for several groups of respondents, that those reporting involvement in a particular illegal act are substantially more approving of that act than those who report no involvement."

Thus, according to Hindelang, there is no need to postulate temporary "techniques of neutralization" of conventional values (Sykes and Matza, 1957) or "drift" (episodic release from moral constraint; Matza,

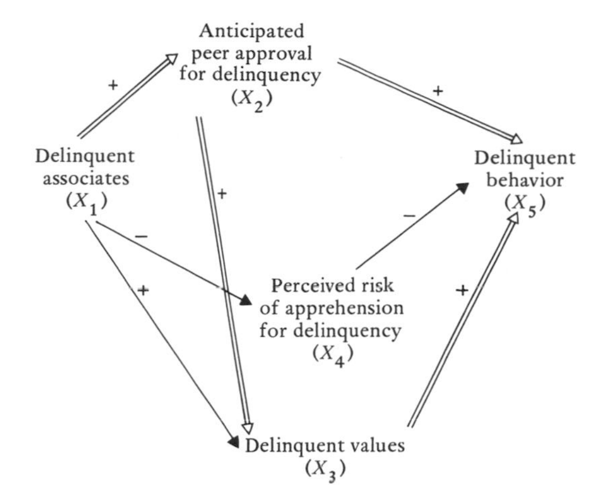

Figure 3.9. The model with perceived risk of apprehension

1964). Hindelang's data indicate a more generalized release from moral constraint independent of extenuating circumstances, which the present model would explain as at least partly caused by lessened attachment to parents or school.

The more troublesome question about the role of delinquent values is one of causal ordering. Do personal attitudes and outlooks regarding certain behaviors precede or result from the degree of participation in those behaviors? Because of their cross-sectional nature, the data are unclear on this point. Liska (1973) claims to show that the causal direction is dependent upon the types of offense, but the data are far from conclusive. In a very small-scale longitudinal analysis, Gold (1963:180) finds evidence "that the factors present in the psychological structure of repeated delinquents were present before they became officially delinquent." And if delinquent values precede official labeling as delinquent, they certainly precede undetected delinquent behavior. It would be naive to claim that values are unaffected by behavior,[8] but the model assumes a priori that the causal ordering is primarily from delinquent values to delinquent behavior. This assumption is especially warranted if one conceives of the theory as outlining initial causes of primary deviance rather than of delinquent role careers.

Delinquent values are not simply the result of parent and school attachments and other exogenous variables, however, They are also one of the mediating factors between delinquent associates and delinquent behavior (see Figure 3.9). Currently there are many unanswered questions surrounding the role of peer group pressures in delinquent behavior. The model's formulation includes three paths from delinquent associates to delinquent behavior, one of which entails delinquent values.

It is reasonable to presume that the adolescent's extent of delinquent associates and his or her degree of acceptance of delinquent values covary. There should be at least a spurious relationship because of the prior influence of attachments on both. The delinquency of values and associations are in fact related (Short and Strodtbeck, 1965; Liska, 1973; Ageton and Elliott, 1974; Hepburn, 1976). Moreover, because adolescents will tend to congregate in groups with already similar values and similar degrees of delinquent involvement, one should not expect a dramatic shift in either delinquent personal values or choice of delinquent associates because of the other.

Assuming that the correlation between delinquent associates and delinquent values is both spurious and causal, what is the main direction of effects between the two variables, to the extent that one does affect the other? Liska (1973) and Hepburn (1976) opt for the causal priority of values, although neither offers data that preclude the reverse ordering, as depicted in Figure 3.9.

Clearly, when an adolescent friendship is formed, there is generally a high degree of value similarity between the participants. But this similarity does not mean that each person's internal values have led him or her to seek friends who have a certain "goodness" or "badness" along a delinquency scale. In fact, each one's involvement in law violation probably remains unexpressed until a certain degree of friendship closeness or rapport is established. If it then becomes apparent that the two differ in their amounts of delinquent behavior, and *if* the less-delinquent adolescent consequently seeks out new friendships, then personal values have directly affected the choice of (non)delinquent associates.

A much more common basis for friendship formation, however, is the perception of similar interests and status within the school setting. Because these factors also relate to delinquency, those who come together as new friends – on the basis of these more-visible school-life features – will usually be similarly involved or uninvolved in law violation. But when differences in delinquent behavior do surface, the friendship is not likely to be terminated because of them. There remains the original similarity in interests, as well as the social ranking system in every school, which severely limits the range of friendship possibilities, to keep the friendship intact.

Adolescents in America are not easily shocked by the discovery that their friends are somewhat more or less delinquent than they are. And even when that shock occurs, it is not an easy task simply to go out and make new friends. It is much easier and more common to learn to live with the new information about a friend's behavior. Consequently, it seems reasonable that the prime causal effect is from delinquent associates to delinquent values. The more involved an individual's friends are in delinquent acts, the more acceptable those acts become to that individual. This follows directly from cognitive-balance reasoning, as it is a dissonant state to associate with delinquent friends while disapproving of their delinquency. And changing a view on the acceptability of certain acts is easier than discarding one friend for another.

The degree of acceptance of delinquent acts may be somewhat situational because of the influence of another variable in Figure 3.9. Delinquent associates directly influence delinquent values, but they primarily are expected to affect values through anticipated peer approval for delinquency. It seems as though there is a relatively common shared misunderstanding among adolescents that delinquent behavior is situationally expected and/or approved by their associates (Matza, 1964; Linden, 1974). In other words, delinquent acts may seem more acceptable in the group context than they appear to be in isolation. Short and Strodtbeck (1965), for example, find that gang boys accord greater prestige to conventional middle-class behavior than to delinquent acts. But these middle-class ways are merely "correct" in general, not in the group setting. In sum, associating with peers who are more involved in delinquent behavior tends to cause the adolescent to become more accepting of delinquent acts in a general sense and, more importantly, tends to cause him or her more often to expect peer approval for committing law violations.

Other than through influencing delinquent behavior via delinquent values in the ways just listed, having delinquent friends and therefore anticipating their approval for law violation has a more direct influence on law violation. That is, that the youth expects social rewards for deviating – whether or not he or she views the act as acceptable – is a powerful force in provoking delinquent behavior. And, of course, the same adolescents who find themselves in this situation are already freer from deviance-preventing attachments. As indicated by the double arrow in Figure 3.9, this search for peer approval (status, "rep") is thought to be the most powerful influence of delinquent associates in generating delinquent conduct. Of course, an adolescent with very nondelinquent associates expects very little approval for misbehavior and is in that situation in the first place because of prior ties to parents and school. So associations and controls are indeed complementary components of the overall scheme.

A third manner in which delinquent associates influence delinquent behavior is by altering the perceived risk of apprehension for delinquency. In spite of the lack in the major theoretical orientations of clear implications about the role of perceived risk of apprehension, it seems plausible that having delinquent associates influences the adolescent's perception of the risk of apprehension in a given situation, which in turn affects the likelihood of delinquent participation. As indicated in Chapter 2, the perceived *certainty* of getting caught seems especially relevant to deterrence. There are at least two ways in which delinquent associates can influence such perceptions. First, almost all delinquent acts go undetected (cf. Williams and Gold, 1972). Therefore, the more the adolescent is with people who have committed delinquent acts, the more likely he or she is to be aware of how often they get away with them. Hence, it appears safer to take the risk. Second, being in the presence of peers in a situation involving potential law violation may confer a safety-in-numbers feeling on the candidate for deviance.[9] Such perceptions of risk may determine the final outcome in a given situation, even controlling for other variables, such as attachments, values, and so forth.

Of course, the adolescent's own experience of getting away with delinquent behavior can "feed back" upon risk perceptions. However, to maintain a recursive, testable model, it must be assumed that the more powerful causal effect is from perceived risk to delinquent behavior. Again it is helpful to conceive of the model as depicting the factors involved in generating the probability or extent of early experimenting with illegal activities. Other feedbacks – including labeling notions – are important in the etiology of delinquent careers, but delinquent careers must start somewhere, and that starting point is what this formulation is most concerned with.[10]

Likewise, there is doubtless some degree of bidirectional causation between delinquent behavior and delinquent associates. As reviewed in

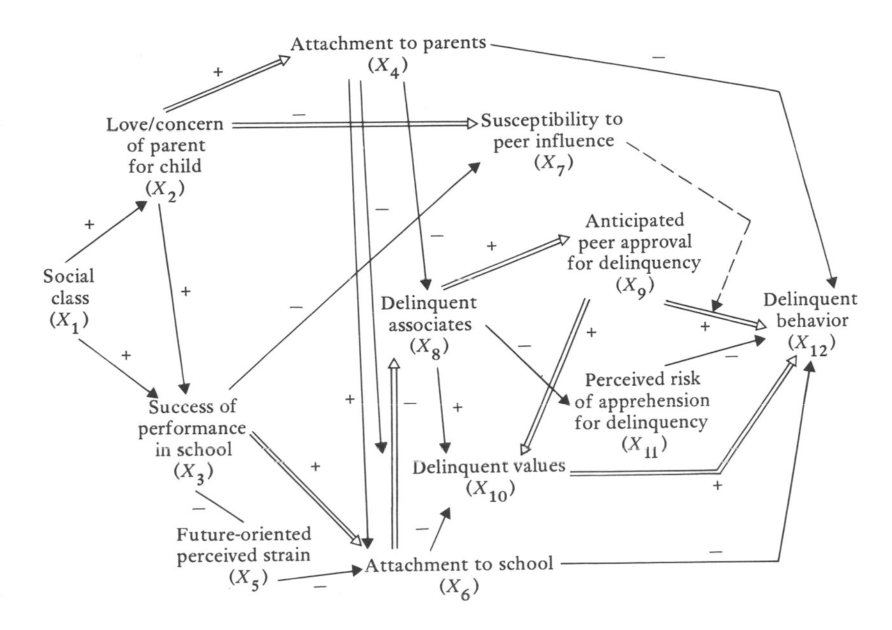

Figure 3.10. The complete theoretical model

Chapter 2, the two variables are highly correlated (cf. Schoenberg, 1975:77). Admittedly, the direction of causality is problematic (cf. Empey and Lubeck, 1971*a* and 1971*b*). But, once again, it will be assumed that the primary influence is from associates to behavior, and the reader should recall that the model attempts to explain the extent or probability of primary deviance.

It is now time to combine all of the fragments of the model and add one more variable to complete the theoretical construction. Figure 3.10 represents the summation of all previous arguments with the addition of susceptibility to peer influence. The inclusion of this concept is based upon the earlier discussion of the salience of self-esteem. The original key to avoiding delinquent values, associates, and involvement lies in the forming of attachments to conventional society. And the mechanism of attachment formation is the development of self-esteem through rewarding relationships with parents and school – the two prime symbols of conformity. But what if the adolescent does not receive positive feedback from parents or school? Does the desire for approval die out, or does he or she turn elsewhere in search of self-worth?

It is assumed that all individuals have the desire to feel important, to feel good about themselves, to be successful at something. Adolescents are probably more susceptible than most to these desires, as they are trying to discover and carve out their identities. Some succeed with their parents or in school. They not only have higher stakes in conformity and are therefore less likely to have delinquent associates, they also are less likely to feel the need to do anything to gain the approval of peers. Lower felt need for peer approval translates into less responsiveness to peer pressure or less susceptibility to peer influence. It is all a matter of degree, and many will depend greatly on peers for "rep," status, or approval. But it seems reasonable that those without any "rep" or status at home or school will be that much more likely to feel the need for peer approval (cf. Hewitt, 1970:68, 75-6, 144 ff.).[11] Thus in Figure 3.10 there are inverse effects of esteem-building parental love and school success on susceptibility to peer influence, with parents presumed to be most salient in determining feelings of general worth.

But susceptibility to peer influence in and of itself need not produce delinquency. Its effect depends on the deviance or conformity of the peers whose approval is sought. Hence, there is an interaction in the model (the dashed arrow leading into another arrow instead of into a construct). That is, the condition of being more susceptible to peer pressure will exacerbate the delinquency-generating power of anticipating approval of law violation from delinquent associates. Given that two people anticipate peer approval consequent to an act, the one who feels the greater need for that reward will be more likely to commit the act.

The implication of the model is, however, that susceptibility to peer influence will be spuriously correlated with anticipating peer approval for delinquent acts. Those having relatively weak ties to conventional society will also experience greater anxiety about their self-worth, and they will tend to flock together with others who are similarly less controlled from deviance, more accepting of illegalities, and more willing to do anything to gain status in the peer group.

There are few studies bearing directly on the issue of susceptibility to peer influence. Yet some indirect support is available. Jensen (1973) reports that an inverse correlation between overall adolescent self-esteem and delinquency is greater given the condition of high parental support. Construing parental support as a conventional source of self-esteem for the offspring, delinquency is most controlled by a quantum of self-esteem that is derived in large proportion from this particular conventional source. The same level of self-esteem, but with more of it derived elsewhere, does less to prevent delinquency. Of course, this is a very speculative interpretation. It may be that the delinquency itself "feeds back" to do more damage to the self-concepts of those closer to their parents, whose disapproval of their actions cuts deeper than the disapproval of a distant, nonsuppportive parent. At the least, these data are not inconsistent with the theoretical formulation.

Another study (Frease, 1973) finds that bad grades in school lead to perceptions that "others think I am a delinquent," even though there is no record of delinquent behavior. The poor student already feels "bad" or "delinquent" ("labeled") and undoubtedly feels a need for status somewhere. He or she is a likely candidate for increased felt need for peer approval and greater susceptibility to peer influence. Once again, however, support for the proposition is more theoretical than empirical.

Finally, Schwendinger's (1963) "instrumental theory of delinquency," as delineated and amplified by Weis (1973), provides a somewhat parallel line of reasoning. The theory focuses primarily on the adolescent social world as most causally immediate in delinquency. Within that world, there exists a "noninclusive sphere of adolescent status arrangements," characterized by a consumption-oriented system of invidious comparisons. That is, among these "strata adolescents" there is a constant competition for social status, and virtually everything becomes a commodity to be exchanged. Strata adolescents are therefore more likely to commit delinquent acts, partly because of their tremendous peer orientation and seeming willingness to do whatever is necessary to climb to the top of the adolescent status ladder. To quote Weis (1973: 325), strata youth are "gratified only within a group, will do anything to please this audience, and all other values depend upon the attainment of this end."

The outsiders, or nonstrata adolescents, do in fact commit fewer delinquent acts (Weis, 1973:429). The main reason seems to be that nonstrata adolescents experience less felt need for peer approval than do the insiders. It is simply not so important to some youth to succeed in the competition for prestige in the adolescent social world. They are less susceptible to peer influence. But what factors produce a nonstrata individual? It seems that the identities of nonstrata youths "are usually established outside the school and the adolescent social world within the family" (Weis, 1973:314). Or, it seems that school-derived self-esteem keeps such nonstrata types as scholars and athletes out of the peer group marketplace. Even within the strata world, the reason given for unexpectedly low delinquency among a particular type of girls seems to be greater school attachment (Weis, 1973:442).

In sum, there is an entire delinquency theory, centered around the crucial role of adolescent identity formation, that yields predictions and empirical results consistent with the notion of variable susceptibility to peer influence. Those adolescents who are unable to ground their identities (derive self-esteem) in school-related successes or family-related experiences are thereby more susceptible to peer influence. And doing whatever is called for to gain prestige in an adolescent peer group can often mean committing delinquent acts.

The theoretical formulation is now complete. It is based on numerous empirical findings and incorporates causal processes from apparently widely divergent orientations. It can be characterized as an "attachment" brand of control theory, but it also includes an appreciation for the roles in generating delinquent behavior of class, strain, peers, values, and perceived risks. It could also be tagged as a brand of differential association theory that includes a place for social controls and so forth. Indeed, perhaps one of its greatest assets is the difficulty in naming it. It is truly a step in the direction of integrating many prominent, often competing, conceptions into one testable formulation. The next step is to put it to the test. Chapter 4 will describe the methods of data collection, measurement, and analysis upon which the test will be based.

4. Methods and measures

The data to be used to test the model were produced by means of a self-administered anonymous questionnaire. The instrument was completed by 734 sophomores in three Seattle, Washington, high schools during April 1975.

Sampling procedures

Because the purpose of this research is analytic rather than descriptive, the crucial sampling criterion was to obtain a sufficient amount of variation in key variables, rather than to represent Seattle or American adolescents. More specifically, the primary concern was to obtain an adequate number of underclass youth in order to test the class-related hypotheses delineated in Chapters 2 and 3. It was felt that sufficient variation along the other dimensions would be easily obtained and not precluded by oversampling areas of lower social class composition.

The basic sampling unit was a high school attendance area. Of the schools within below-median-income areas, three were sampled on the bases of social class and racial composition and accessibility. An effort was made to ensure that the possible effects of underclass membership would not be confounded with the effects of a particular racial or ethnic status. In fact, a relative independence of race and social class was achieved, as shown in Table 4.1.

Although the sampling was successful in obtaining a racially mixed underclass (and racial subgroups heterogeneous by social class), the absolute numbers of black and underclass subjects are exceedingly low. This is partly because of Seattle's lack of a hard-core slum area and partly because of sampling. But it should be restated that this research is not an attempt to describe or represent particular populations of youth. It is a search for causal relations. The absence of any given subtype of adolescent in the overall sample (blacks, for example) challenges only the external validity or generalizability of the causal process-

Table 4.1. *Percentage underclass by race*

Race of respondent	% classified as underclass
White ($N = 518$)	7.9 ($N = 41$)
Asian ($N = 114$)	8.0 ($N = 9$)
Black ($N = 60$)	6.7 ($N = 4$)
Other/nonresponse ($N = 42$)	9.5 ($N = 4$)
Total ($N = 734$)	7.9 ($N = 58$)

es apparently operating among the types of adolescents studied, something that is easy to check with future samples. The lack of representative sampling does not threaten the internal validity of the tests for the tenability of the model *as it applies to those sampled.*

Tenth graders were chosen because they have reached the ages of peak delinquent involvement (fifteen to sixteen years), yet they are less likely than older adolescents to have dropped out of school or to have become involved in careers of secondary deviance. In other words, students at this age should provide the widest possible range of delinquent behavior without an extensive amount of feedback from the labeling effects of official delinquency. Thus age is controlled by means of homogeneous sampling throughout the analysis, as 93 percent of all respondents are fifteen or sixteen years old. It is assumed a priori that similar causal processes operate in generating delinquent behavior from very early adolescence (age eleven or twelve) until the youth forms other bonds or attachments not included in the model (such as higher education, full-time employment, marriage). But, of course, the question of extendability of results along the age continuum is an issue for empirical research beyond the scope of this study.

The questionnaire was administered within one school period, ranging from fifty to sixty minutes. Virtually all respondents had ample time to complete the instrument. Only 18 of 734 questionnaires were incomplete because of nonresponse to the final items. Those who failed to complete the instrument did not differ in any other discernible way from the other subjects, so their data were retained in all analyses for which responses were provided. Students were assured of anonymity and were encouraged to ask the administrator for private assistance in understanding or responding to any particular item. Each respondent was allowed to place his or her own completed questionnaire in a box already containing other completed questionnaires. Those who finished early were required to remain quietly in their seats and engage in personal study. Thus there was little incentive to hurry through the instrument haphazardly to get out of class.

In sum, the sample consists of approximately two-thirds of the sophomores enrolled in three high schools located in relatively poor (but by no means ghetto or slum) areas of Seattle.[1] If the research goals were to describe the amount of school attachment or delinquent behavior among the city's adolescents, the data might be misleading. Those who were in school and in class would probably show greater average school attachment and less delinquent involvement than those absent (not to mention those institutionalized elsewhere for misbehavior).

In the search for associations and influences, however, the primary concern is with the amount of variation along key dimensions. There can be no evidence of correlation or causation without variation. The sample is satisfactory in that it does provide the necessary variations. Furthermore, any sampling-imposed confinement on the variances of the constructs will likely have a tempering effect on conclusions. That is, less variation tends to attenuate coefficients, so that associations that appear to be strong in spite of such circumstances are based on more solid ground because of those very conditions. Thus it is unlikely that the sampling design will contribute to making rash causal assertions based on flimsy empirical footing.

The following sections describe the measures employed to indicate the theoretical constructs in the model (see Figure 3.10).

Measures of social class

As discussed in Chapters 2 and 3, it is possible that the manner in which social class is measured will make some difference in substantive conclusions. Specifically, class is more likely to be found causally relevant to delinquent behavior if it is measured by underclass/earning-class criteria than if it is measured by the common stepladder of father's occupation categories. Class will be measured here in both ways in order (*a*) to compare the results of the father's occupation categories with those of

Table 4.2. *Distribution of present sample and Hirschi's sample by father's occupation*

Father's occupation	% of present sample	% of Hirschi's
1. Unskilled labor	10	13
2. Semiskilled labor	19	14
3. Skilled manual	32	35
4. White collar	14	13
5. Professional/ executive	26	25
Total	101%[a] (N = 581[b])	100% (N = 1121)

[a]The percentages do not sum to 100 here and in some following tables because of rounding.
[b]The total number of students will vary from table to table because of different response rates for almost every item in the questionnaire. Students for whom all data in a table are not available are excluded from that particular table. In this case, 153 students (734 minus 581) failed to provide adequate information on their father's occupations. This typically high rate of nonresponse for such a measure is one of the criticisms of a father's-occupation measurement of social class mentioned in Chapter 2.

other studies employing similar measures, (*b*) to test the tenability of underclass/earning-class effects in the model, and (*c*) to gain insight into the influence of measurement techniques on substantive conclusions.

There are many ways of dividing father's occupation into SES categories in the literature. Each has advantages and drawbacks. This research employs Hirschi's (1969:69, 265–6) technique, primarily for the opportunity it entails for comparison or replication. That is, Hirschi's sample seems to be quite similar to this one – primarily earning-class school attenders.

Basically, respondents were asked to name and briefly describe each parent's job. With this information I coded the letter corresponding to the correct job type from a previously prepared list.[2]

Table 4.2 shows the distribution of respondents among the five SES categories named by Hirschi (1969). Also included are the corresponding percentages from Hirschi's sample to demonstrate the similarity in SES composition of the two samples, in anticipation of replicating Hirschi's SES findings.

An alternative measure of social class is an underclass/earning-class dichotomy (UC/EC). Every student was placed in one of the two classes in the manner described here.

Students who reported their parents' total income as "poverty level" or "somewhat below average" were included in the pool of possible underclass membership. Reports of average to wealthy income, as well as failure to respond to the income item, resulted in exclusion from underclass possibility. Thus, throughout the classification procedure, no one was allowed to become underclass by default. Consistent evidence of low life chances had to be provided in order for a student to be categorized as underclass. The primary goal was to obtain a pure underclass group uncontaminated by children of regular earners. Any classification errors should be in the direction of mixing a few underclass students into the much larger earning-class group.

The income-based pool of possible underclass included 109 (of 734) students.[3] To remain in the underclass, students had to supply evidence of either the family's receipt of welfare benefits or the father's recent or present unemployment. For those without fathers, the mother's recent or present unemployment was the relevant criterion. These requirements for underclass membership pared the pool from 109 to 80. Once again, the relatively few who failed to respond to these items became earning class by default. Already the underclass was quite pure, as regular workers who had not received welfare were excluded even if the family's income was perceived as poverty level.

Finally, as a check against a combination of misperception of family income and very liberal interpretation of "unemployed," another criterion was added. In order to remain underclass, students had to supply information that both parents had not graduated from college *or*[4] that both parents were not white-collar or professional/executive employees. Thus the temporarily laid-off engineer or teacher did not qualify as a member of the theoretical underclass.

The net result is that 58 of the 734 students were deemed to come from underclass families. As was shown in Table 4.1, they were quite evenly distributed by race. The limited variation in social class (UC/EC) as an independent variable will most likely serve to attenuate its apparent effects on other variables. In this sense, the current study may be nearly as guilty as some past studies (see Chapter 2) of not giving class a fair chance to demonstrate its causal efficacy.

Measures of parental influences

The theoretical construct of parental love for the child is central to the model, especially as it has generated degrees of parent-derived self-esteem within the offspring. The indicators are questionnaire items dealing with how *past* mother and father treatments led the adolescent to feel about him- or herself (positive and loved, or negative and unloved). The students' perceptions in this regard were presumed to reflect degrees of parental love or concern. Students were asked to respond to six items concerning their fathers and six parallel items concerning their mothers. The items listed here are numbered by questionnaire location, for comparisons with the Appendix and with later factor analyses. Scores were assigned as follows in a manner similar to that employed by Nye (1958).[5]

31./41 It has been hard for me to please my (father/mother). Always (0) Usually (0) Sometimes (0) Seldom (1) Never (2)

32./42 My (father/mother) has praised me when I've done a good job at something. Always (2) Usually (1) Sometimes (0) Seldom (0) Never (0)

33./43 My (father/mother) has ridiculed or made fun of my ideas. Always (0) Usually (0) Sometimes (0) Seldom (1) Never (2)

34./44 My (father/mother) has trusted me. Always (2) Usually (1) Sometimes (0) Seldom (0) Never (0)

35./45 My (father/mother) has shown respect for my opinions and feelings. Always (2) Usually (1) Sometimes (0) Seldom (0) Never (0)

36./46 My (father/mother) has seemed to wish I were a different type of person. Always (0) Usually (0) Sometimes (0) Seldom (1) Never (2)

As the reader can see, the questions are all worded in the past (in contrast to present parent-attachment items), and they are worded in opposite directions to avoid a response set bias. That is, a response of "always" sometimes indicates low parental love (zero) and other times signifies high parental love (two).

In a similar manner, items were included in the questionnaire to indicate current attachment to mother and father (separately). In the case of having no one acting as father or mother, the student received a zero level of attachment to that parent. All other parent-attachment items were scored as the parental-love items – two for the most-attached response, one for the next most attached, and zero for all others. The reader is referred to the Appendix for details of the response alternatives contained in the questionnaire.

The following items (numbered by questionnaire location) were meant to measure parental attachment:

20./24 Is your (father/mother) living at home with you?
22./26 Do you care what your (father/mother) thinks of you?
27./29 I'm closer to my (father/mother) than are most people my age.
28./30 As an adult, I want to live near where my (father/mother) will be living.
37./47 When I have problems I confide in my (father/mother).
38./48 I feel angry or rebellious toward my (father/mother).
39./49 When I have free time I spend it with my (father/mother).
40./50 In my free time away from home, my (father/mother) knows whom I'm with and where I am.

The multiple items relating to parents were intended to measure four separate dimensions: father love, father attachment, mother love, and mother attachment. Factor analysis was employed to determine if separate dimensions were indeed measured and to refine the resulting indexes. Of perhaps greatest concern was the possibility of multicollinearity (that is, not having as many dimensions as are supposed) between the same-parent love and attachment constructs. If the two variables are too highly related, estimates of their separate effects will be difficult to determine and plagued by very high sensitivity to sampling and measurement errors (Blalock, 1972:456–7).

Initially, all parent items were included in a "principal factoring with iteration" factor analysis (type PA2 in Nie et al., 1975:480) with oblique rotation. The only interpretable results were that mother and father items tended to load on the first two factors, respectively. Hence, separate factor analyses were carried out for the mother items and the father items.

All the father items were then included in the same factor analysis with the request that only two factors be extracted in accordance with the theoretical base. The results generally confirmed initial notions of the face validity of the individual items as indicators of the proper constructs. Table 4.3 represents the factor loadings from the obliquely ro-

Table 4.3. *Loadings on obliquely rotated factors of father-related items*

Construct that item was meant to measure	Questionnaire item number	Factor 1: attachment	Factor 2: love
Father love	31[a]	.03	.76
	32	.40	.26
	33[a]	.01	.66
	34[a]	.32	.44
	35	.48	.38
	36[a]	.03	.81
Father attachment	22	.38	.25
	27[a]	.68	.12
	28[a]	.52	.05
	37[a]	.62	.08
	38	.17	.58
	39[a]	.67	.06
	40	.45	.13

Note: Negative signs were dropped from some of the loadings here and in all the following factor analysis tables, as they merely reflect the "direction" of the wording of questionnaire items. Of course, all signs were checked to be sure that they matched the intended direction of the item.
[a]Items retained as part of final index.

tated factor-pattern matrix for the father items listed according to questionnaire location. The parallel data for mother-related items appear in Table 4.4.

On the bases of Tables 4.3 and 4.4, several items were excluded from further utilization in composite indexes of father or mother love and attachment. A prerequisite was to retain parallel items for father and mother indexes. Those items that failed to load distinctly on one factor for both parents, or that loaded on the "wrong" factor relative to expectations for either parent, were discarded. For example, father item thirty-five (showing respect for child's feelings) loaded too heavily (.48) on attachment to be considered a distinct measure of the love dimension. Accordingly, item thirty-five (and the corresponding item forty-five for mother) were dropped from the love indexes, even though the item loaded quite satisfactorily for mothers – .67 on love and .17 on attachment. In another example, parallel items thirty-eight and forty-eight (feeling angry or rebellious toward the parent) loaded on the "wrong" dimension. Intended to measure current attachment, they ap-

Table 4.4. *Loadings on obliquely rotated factors of mother-related items*

Construct that item was meant to measure	Questionnaire item number	Factor 1: attachment	Factor 2: love
Mother love	41[a]	.08	.65
	42	.28	.34
	43[a]	.15	.71
	44[a]	.12	.67
	45	.17	.67
	46[a]	.04	.76
Mother attachment	26	.25	.36
	29[a]	.61	.16
	30[a]	.53	.04
	47[a]	.69	.07
	48	.13	.54
	49[a]	.79	.10
	50	.46	.02

Note: Actually, the love factor was extracted first from the mother data, rather than the attachment factor, as with the father items. The first factor extracted is the one that alone accounts for the greatest amount of variation among items.
[a]Items retained as part of final index.

peared to be more strongly influenced by perceptions of past parental treatment. Hence, they were dropped.

The items retained in the indexes are noted in Tables 4.3 and 4.4. The attachment indexes also include items nineteen and twenty for the father and twenty-three and twenty-four for the mother, which were not included in the factor analysis. They deal with having a parent and whether the parent lives at home. The results are parallel four-item indexes for mother love and father love, and six-item indexes for mother attachment and father attachment. According to traditional reliability theory, estimates of the reliabilities of sets of items can be obtained from the formula

$$r_{kk} = \frac{k\bar{r}_{ij}}{1 + (k - 1)\bar{r}_{ij}},$$

where r_{kk} = the reliability of the set of items, k = the number of items in the set, and $\bar{r}_{ij}$ = the mean correlation between pairs of items in the set. This yields estimates of .79 for the reliabilities of the father-love and mother-love indexes, .78 for mother attachment, and .77 for father attachment. Thus measurement error may attenuate or distort "true" relationships and effects, but to similar degrees for these various constructs, so as not to confuse causal interpretations unduly.

As for the issue of multicollinearity between love and attachment, the factor loadings in Tables 4.3 and 4.4 show that separate dimensions apparently do exist. But, conversely, the separate dimensions (or factors) are also quite highly related. Using oblique rotations, the love and attachment factors were correlated at .56 for fathers and .67 for mothers.[6] It appears that there is at least as much empirical evidence for retaining distinct theoretical constructs as there is for grouping love and attachment in one conglomerate parent variable. And it is more satisfying conceptually to keep the concepts separated; so such a separation will be maintained.

The final consideration in measuring parent-related phenomena involves moving from separate mother and father scores to overall parental-love and attachment-to-parents indexes. Such a procedure necessitates that some assumptions be made about the substantive nature of the influence of these factors on delinquency-related variables. In the extreme, what is the effect of being very highly attached to one parent while virtually unattached to the other (or not having the second parent)? Is this situation more similar to being moderately attached to two parents (so that the attachment scores would add to the same total) or to being very highly attached to both parents (so that the single highest attachment yields the same total)?

My presumption is that the "single highest" model best fits reality. That is, if two adolescents are equally attached to their mothers, with scores of *X*, and less attached to their fathers, by different degrees, it is their mother attachments that provide them with their best reason to conform. They each can be conceptualized as having an *X* amount of stake in conformity. For whatever stakes in conformity may have resulted from their attachments to their fathers are superseded by the stronger attachments to their mothers. The single greatest degree of psychological presence of a parent in a delinquency-tempting situation should be the key to predicting a delinquent or a conforming outcome.

The case against the simple addition of father and mother scores is best shown in the situation of a single-parent adolescent. One fatherless girl may have a strong tie to her mother, say $2T$ in amount, which prevents her from deviating. Another girl may simply have moderate ties of strength *T* to each of two parents. An additive model would result in identical degrees of attachment, whereas in reality the second girl lacks any strong bond to either adult.

The "single greatest" models of parental love and attachment not only make the most sense theoretically but allow for the retention of single-parent students as part of the sample. With any of the four separate parent indexes (father love, for example), students who failed to answer a majority of the individual items were excluded. For those answering a majority but not all of the items, total index scores were derived by extrapolating their response tendencies.[7] That is, a score of eight from only four completed items became a score of twelve on a six-item index. To be excluded from the main parental-love analysis, then, required the literal absence of both parents or the failure to respond to a majority of both father-love and mother-love items. Only six respondents were so excluded, with no respondents being excluded because of missing parent-attachment data.

Measures of the role of the school

Additive indexes of the two school-related constructs were developed from many individual school items in a manner similar to that for the indexes of parent-related variables just described. Questionnaire items one to three and eight to ten were originally intended to measure school success, the theoretical generator of school-related self-esteem. In each case, the most-successful response was scored two, the next one, and the remaining responses zero. The reader is invited to refer to the Appendix for the specific content of the retained items. With the same scoring system, questionnaire items four to seven and eleven to fourteen were intended to measure school attachment. All of the items were included in a principal factor with oblique rotation factor analysis (see Nie et al., 1975:480, 485–6) to determine the independence of the two school dimensions and to aid in the compilation of indexes. Two factors were requested. Results are summarized in Table 4.5.

As with the parent items, some school items were discarded from the final indexes because of "double loading," loading on the "wrong" factor, or not loading highly on either factor. Those retained are noted. The oblique rotation of factors shows a moderately strong interfactor correlation of .43. The reliabilities of the resulting four-item school-success index and the seven-item correlations are .65 and .70, respect-

Table 4.5. *Loadings on obliquely rotated factors of school-related items*

Construct that item was meant to measure	Questionnaire item number	Factor 1: attachment	Factor 2: love
School success	1	.53	.35
	2	.40	.40
	3[a]	.23	.58
	8[a]	.12	.38
	9[a]	.41	.75
	10[a]	.48	.54
School attachment	4[a]	.46	.26
	5[a]	.54	.19
	6	.31	.06
	7[a]	.47	.22
	11[a]	.58	.26
	12[a]	.46	.27
	13[a]	.53	.19
	14[a]	.46	.35

[a] Items retained as part of final indexes.

ively. Once again, measurement error should attenuate relationships, but not differently, because of similar reliabilities.

Measures of strain

As discussed quite extensively in Chapter 2, it appears that a valid measure of strain is simply the level of realistic occupational expectation. Utilization of such a measure is based on evidence of quite uniform occupational aspirations (hopes, dreams). Thus expectations measure the degree of coming down or expected failure compared to real desires. Furthermore, using expectations alone as an indicator of strain avoids the previously outlined difficulties entailed in using "difference" or "discrepancy" scores between stated aspirations and expectations (see Chapter 2). Aspirations seem to be frequently compromised in light of realistic opportunities *before* being stated in a research instrument (cf. Rodman et al., 1974; Caro and Pihlblad, 1965; Gold, 1963:167).

And apparent effects of aspiration–expectation discrepancies can often "best be accounted for in terms of the additive formulation as a simple inverse function of educational and occupational expectations" (Liska, 1971:105). In short, then, occupational expectations,[8] as categorized in one of the five job-classification types used earlier to measure SES of father's occupation, are one measure of perceived strain. Expectations of professional or executive positions signify low strain, whereas expectations of unskilled labor mark high strain.

Additionally, several alternative measures of strain were developed for the sake of comparison and in search of insights into the effects of measuring techniques upon substantive conclusions. Educational expectations were tapped, utilizing a six-category scale ranging from "some high school or less" to "college plus graduate school." Also, perceptions of barriers to goals were measured (examples of barriers are "lack of money," "lack of ability," "they don't want my kind," etc.). Presumably, a greater number of perceived barriers indicates a greater amount of strain or frustration. Alternatively, a single question – "Do you worry about getting a decent 'life's work' in the future?" – is another likely measure of strain.

Finally, occupational and educational aspirations were measured according to the same scales used for indicating the respective expectations, and discrepancy scores were calculated. But in an effort to avoid some of the inadequacies of simple discrepancy scores in past studies, considerations beyond the mere subtraction of expectation level from aspiration level were included.

A score on an index of occupational discrepancy began with a comparison of aspiration and expectation categories. In requesting aspirations, emphasis was placed on ideal, unencumbered-by-reality desires. The realistic nature of expectations was stressed. Hence, any difference between the two was scored as one to begin the occupational-discrepancy-scale scoring. Regardless of the extent, or even the direction, of the aspiration–expectation discrepancy, the essential feature of a difference was that the student expected to work at a type of job other than that which he or she would have preferred. Of course, no difference between the two was scored zero as the total occupational-discrepancy-index score.

If one or two barriers to desired work were checked, another point of strain was added for those indicating an original discrepancy. Two points were added if three to five barriers were perceived. An index score remained at one (aspiration $\neq$ expectations) if no barriers were checked. But if the student responded, "I just don't care that much" as one reason for failing to expect a desired job, his or her total index score was zero regardless of other responses. The goal was to "purify" strain by attributing strain or frustration only to those who really feel it. Consequently, a student who reported a discrepancy but also noted that he or she really didn't care was judged no more strained than the student who marked several barriers but still expected to attain a desired job.

Additional criteria further refined the discrepancy index of occupational strain. Even if aspirations and expectations failed to coincide and barriers were perceived, the total index score was reduced to zero if the student reported that the desired job was merely a "wild dream," or that he or she had spent no time seriously considering post-high school plans, or that he or she had not worried at all about getting a decent life's work (questionnaire items eighty-six, eighty-seven, and eighty-eight, found in the Appendix). On the other hand, strain points were added for the extreme positive responses to these items, as theoretical strain should be greater for those who have well-thought-out and/or strong desires for unobtainable jobs and/or occupational worries. And finally, because the concern is with strain as a cause rather than a consequence of delinquent behavior, students high on a "labeled" index of official trouble who also perceived barriers, such as "I won't get the breaks" or "They don't want my kind," were excluded from registering nonzero strain. In this way, serious causal feedback from official delinquency to strain was eliminated from the search for *effects* of futuristic strain. The net result is a rather complex index of occupational strain with a possible range of zero to eight (see the Appendix for exact scoring), on which 445 (of 734) students registered zero strain and another sixty-nine failed to supply responses sufficient to acquire a score.

The educational-discrepancy index of strain was likewise based on aspiration–expectation differences. A total score was zero if expectations met or exceeded aspirations on the six-point education scale. But here an excess of aspirations was scored by the degree (in number of categories) to which aspirations exceeded expectations. Thus the basic discrepancy score could reach as high as five, if the student desired graduate school (six) but expected to fail to graduate from high school (one). It was felt that quantitative differences are much more justifiable with years of education than with job types, as educational level more closely approximates an interval scale.

Information on perceived barriers to desired educational level supplemented this index. Once again, a response of "I just don't care that much" reduced the total strain score to zero. One or two perceived barriers added one point to the aspiration–expectation numerical difference, and three to five marked barriers added two scale points. The result is an index of educational-discrepancy strain with a range of zero to seven, on which 473 scored zero and 8 failed to respond (of $N = 734$). As with the occupational-discrepancy measure, these additional qualifications and criteria should reduce the amount of measurement error found in the typical "aspirations minus expectations" indicators. The presumption is that far too much futuristic strain is commonly attributed to adolescents on the basis of simple aspiration and expectation data, with little or no effort to probe feelings of frustration or alternative reasons for the discrepancies.

The present measures of strain, then, include occupational- and educational-discrepancy indexes, occupational and educational expectations, the degree of worrying about a future career, and the number of perceived barriers to satisfactory job and school levels.

Measures of peer influences

In measuring these three theoretical constructs, there is once again (as with parent and school items) the possibility of multicollinearity. Consequently, all of the items intended to measure these peer-related conceptions were included in a single factor analysis to verify conceptual distinctions and to refine final indexes. Questionnaire items 69, 114, and 115 (see the Appendix for the content of retained items) were intended to measure susceptibility to peer influence. Items 70, 72, and 74 were devised to measure the degree of delinquent involvement of associates, and items 75, 76, and 77 were meant to tap anticipated approval of delinquent acts by friends. Table 4.6 summarizes the results of a principal factoring solution with oblique rotation for the requested three factors.

It is evident from Table 4.6 that there is insufficient justification for retaining delinquent associates and anticipated peer approval for delinquency as distinct constructs. Virtually all of the items intended to

Table 4.6. *Loadings on obliquely rotated factors of peer-related items*

Construct that item was meant to measure	Questionnaire item number	Factor 1: delinquent associates	Factor 2: importance of friends	Factor 3: talked into things
Susceptibility	69[a]	.06	.02	.50
to peer influence	114	.04	.34	.04
	115	.13	.29	.11
Delinquent	70	.38	.29	.15
associates	72[a]	.81	.02	.15
	74[a]	.71	.03	.06
Anticipation of	75[a]	.56	.19	.16
peer approval	76[a]	.62	.15	.03
for delinquency	77[a]	.65	.13	.11

[a]Items retained as part of final indexes.

measure these variables load strongly and quite exclusively on the first factor, which seems to represent delinquent associates. It appears that items concerning the expected reactions of friends to a student's delinquent acts are as useful as indicators of having delinquent associates as are more direct queries about the actual behavior of friends.

Excluding anticipation of approval from the model for purposes of empirical testing does not invalidate the underlying reasoning about the manner in which delinquent associates influence delinquent behavior. Indeed, the proposal in Chapter 3 that the primary mechanism of these effects is through anticipations of peer approval for misdeeds is supported by these findings. Anticipated peer approval for delinquency is such an integral aspect of having delinquent friends that it cannot justifiably be separated out for measurement. To say that an adolescent has delinquent friends is to say that he or she anticipates peer approval for delinquent acts.

As usual, the items in Table 4.6 comprising the final indexes are noted. Item seventy is excluded from the new, composite delinquent-associates scale for failing to load as highly as the others and for loading too highly on a separate factor. The resulting five-item index of delinquent associates has a range of zero to thirteen (see the Appendix for exact scoring of responses) and a reliability of .81.

The three items intended to measure susceptibility to peer influence seem instead to be tapping two separate dimensions. In Table 4.6 these have been labeled "importance of friends" and "talked into things." These labels are intended merely to capture succinctly the essence of the items loading highly on the particular factor. Items 114 and 115, dealing with the general importance of friends to an adolescent, have a low loading on factor two. A two-item index based on them would not be very reliable, as their inter-item correlation is low (r = .12). Hence, those items are excluded, leaving item sixty-nine ("Are you ever talked into doing things by your friends that you really don't want to do?") as the single indicator of susceptibility to peer influence. From the factor loadings, it seems to form a relatively distinct dimension. And the obliquely rotated factors one and three are only moderately correlated at .32. But more important, the face validity of item sixty-nine is high. That is, being talked into things easily – be it going to the ballet or to a gang fight – is a reasonable sign of susceptibility to peer influence in an attempt to please and thereby gain the approval of associates.

Measures of deterrence

For reasons detailed in Chapters 2 and 3, the perceived certainty of getting caught will be the focus in testing deterrence notions. Thus the measure of perceived risk is an additive combination of responses to two questionnaire items relating to perceptions of personal chances of getting caught in two hypothetical situations. Scores on each item range from one (very low chance of apprehension) to five (very high chance of apprehension). Hence, the overall index ranges from two to ten, with a reliability of .69.

Measures of delinquency

Rather than merely assuming that delinquent values and delinquent behavior are distinct dimensions amenable to separate measurement, I have included both in this section in order to test that presumption through factor analysis. All of the items intended to measure these conceptions were included in a principal factoring analysis with oblique rotation. No predetermined number of factors was requested. The results appear in Table 4.7. Items retained in the final index are noted; in this case, all items are retained.

It is clear from Table 4.7 that values and behavior are distinct dimen-

Table 4.7. *Loading on obliquely rotated factors of delinquency-related items*

Construct that item was meant to measure	Questionnaire item number	Factor 1: values	Factor 2: behavior (vandalism)	Factor 3: behavior (theft)	Factor 4: behavior (assault)
Delinquent	106[a]	.60	.09	.10	.17
values	107[a]	.64	.11	.09	.07
	108[a]	.63	.07	.02	.00
	109[a]	.71	.02	.05	.10
	110[a]	.55	.03	.15	.32
	111[a]	.49	.03	.18	.04
Delinquent	54[a]	.18	.01	.61	.01
behavior	56[a]	.03	.02	.85	.02
Theft	58[a]	.06	.16	.43	.21
	64[a]	.17	.03	.14[b]	.06
Vandalism	60[a]	.05	.78	.00	.08
	62[a]	.01	.85	.02	.04
Assault	66[a]	.02	.02	.08	.72
	67[a]	.04	.05	.06	.57

[a]Items retained as part of final indexes.
[b]This loading is quite low, but item sixty-four (car theft) is included under theft on the basis of face validity.

sions. All of the value items load quite highly and exclusively on factor one. Few of the behavior items load on factor one beyond a negligible degree. And factor one's correlation with the other obliquely rotated factors range from .22 to .38. Accordingly, the measure of delinquent values is a six-item index with a range of zero to seventeen (see the Appendix for exact scoring of responses). The reliability of the index, based on inter-item correlations, is .80 – quite strong and quite similar to the reliabilities of other indexes.

The final measurement consideration relates to the dependent variable. As the focus of the entire analysis, delinquent behavior must be measured in a valid and reliable manner. Before examining the details of the loadings of specific delinquency items in the factor analysis represented in Table 4.7, then, it would be useful first to discuss more general concerns about self-reported delinquency measurement procedures.

As stated in Chapter 2, the theoretical variable delinquent behavior refers to a continuum of actual behavior of adolescents. Behavior is what the traditional orientations are attempting to explain, and behavior is what the present model is attempting to explain. Yet very seldom is behavior directly observed in sociological analyses. And with illegal behavior, which the actors have an incentive to keep hidden from outside observation, the difficulties with direct observation on any large scale are insurmountable. Thus researchers must necessarily rely on the reports of others for information. A basic decision in any study of adolescent illegal conduct is whether to rely upon the records of official social control agencies or to survey the adolescents themselves regarding their misdeeds.

The inadequacies of official delinquency statistics are well known to serious students of the subject and need not be discussed at length here. Briefly, having been labeled as a delinquent by society's officials is a status and not a measure of actual behavior. Official records are, of course, useful in the study of the processes entailed in the juvenile justice system, but they are too far removed from behavior to serve as measures of delinquent behavior. As Williams and Gold's (1972) national sample reveals, less than 3 percent of admitted juvenile offenses are known to the police. Williams and Gold (1972:226) conclude that "official measures of delinquency do not accurately reflect delinquent behavior" (cf. Schoenberg, 1975:98; Erickson, 1972:389).

Researchers are left in the somewhat uncomfortable position of relying on the words of the adolescents for a measure of their misdeeds. Laymen and skilled critics alike are quick to point out the possibility of dishonest or otherwise erroneous responses. The data are undoubtedly obscured by instances of concealment, exaggeration, and forgetfulness. But so far, at least, the many self-report studies fail to show evidence of a correlation of any of these types of error with other relevant variables. At this point it is justifiable to say that self-reports seem to be the best available data source for delinquent behavior and that measurement errors do not appear to be sufficiently correlated with other variables to bias interpretations. In fact, several tests of the validity and/or reliability of self-reported delinquency instruments have come up with rather favorable results, including checks against lie detectors, official records, and the word of informants (cf. Dentler's remarks in Hardt and Bodine, 1965:18; Clark and Tifft, 1966; Gold, 1966; Erickson, 1972; Farrington, 1973; Hood and Sparks, 1970:64–70; Blackmore, 1974; Gould, 1969).

In an extensive recent analysis of self-report methodology, Hardt and

Peterson-Hardt (1977) conclude that the procedure "yields accurate responses and can make an important contribution to etiological studies of delinquent behavior" (pp. 255–6). And even in the literature focusing on the general controversy over the consistency between attitudes and behavior, self-reported deviance is employed to measure the behavior dimension (Albrecht and Carpenter, 1976) and is cited by critics of questionnaires as one example of relatively valid questionnaire measurement (Deutscher, 1966). Liska (1974) concludes that strong criticism leveled by some against the use of questionnaires as a measure of overt behavior "is not empirically justified" (p. 263).

There remain many possible variations in procedure under the general heading of self-reported delinquency measures. In the first place, the present measure will include only illegal, criminal, or chargeable offenses. Trivial misbehaviors are excluded as obscuring the conception of the dependent variable, as are so-called status offenses, for which juveniles but not adults may be legally apprehended. Schoenberg (1975: 129), for example, reports that "A distinction between self-reported criminal offenses and self-reported status offenses was found to be empirically justified." Status offenses are not studied in this research, but the assumption is that the processes generating involvement in status offenses are similar to those delineated as leading to illegal behavior. In other words, the model depicts influences on the willingness of an adolescent to break rules, regardless of the specific type of deviation. Specific illegal offenses are easier to measure accurately and are more substantively interesting than more vague and trivial status offenses.

The general format of the survey is another major variation among self-report studies. The choice is between interviews or anonymous questionnaires. Gold (in Gold and Voss, 1967:116) feels that the ability to probe in an interview situation enables the researcher "to measure better what we mean by delinquency despite the problem of concealment inherent in a breakdown of anonymity." That is, checklist data are thought by some to encourage more careless responses with little guard against exaggerations or forgetfulness. However, concealment can be quite a serious difficulty in a face-to-face interview situation. Because of the problem of concealment or other biases in interviews, as well as the advantages of low cost and practical ease of collecting data by questionnaires, anonymous group-administered questionnaires were used in this study.

Yet the problems of forgetfulness and exaggeration were not ignored.

To counter extensive memory errors, the time frame of the items was limited to the past year.[9] Students should be able to remember or estimate the number of times they have committed specific offenses within such a specific and relatively short time span without the prodding of an interviewer. To guard against exaggeration or overreporting of trivia, each self-report item was followed by a probe for details. Students were asked to describe briefly the last such incident. This request was meant to encourage them to think twice about the accuracy of the number of offenses they reported, and it enabled the researcher to exclude trivial or nonsense responses. In sum, the advantage of guaranteed anonymity is combined with features designed to counteract the relative inadequacies of the self-administered questionnaire format.

Another major variation in self-report measurement is the distinction between *frequency* and *seriousness* of delinquent behavior. It probably makes very little difference which way such behavior is measured. That is, frequency and seriousness are probably highly related to one another. More importantly, they probably are similarly related to and similarly "caused by" other variables. Gold (1966) and Williams and Gold (1972) report findings generally confirming these suppositions. To be safe and to compare the results from different measures, however, measures of both dimensions have been devised. But the primary analysis will employ frequency of delinquent behavior (within the past year) as the dependent variable. Frequencies simply have greater face validity and ease of interpretation than do seriousness weightings.

The measure of frequency consists of the simple addition of the number of times the respondent reports having committed each of eight acts within the past year. The offenses include small theft, medium theft, large theft, car theft, medium property destruction, large property destruction, interpersonal violence, and attacking someone with a weapon (see the section on delinquent behavior in the Appendix, items fifty-four, fifty-six, fifty-eight, sixty, sixty-two, sixty-four, sixty-six, and sixty-seven). Each offense is scored with the exact reported number of commissions up to and including ten. All admissions of eleven or more commissions of a single offense are coded as twenty. It was felt that recollection of more than ten specific occasions is highly unlikely, so that most higher numbers are merely individual students' ways of saying "many times," which is arbitrarily given twice the delinquent behavior weight as ten admitted commissions. The eight-item index of fre

Table 4.8. *Distribution of scores along the frequency-of-delinquency index*

Index score (total admissions of 8 offenses)	Number of respondents (% of total sample in parentheses)
0	341 (48%[a])
1	92 (13%)
2	49 (7%)
3	48 (7%)
4	26 (4%)
5	23 (3%)
6	12 (2%)
7	12 (2%)
8	11 (2%)
9	2 (0%)
10	6 (1%)
11-20	40 (6%)
21-30	28 (4%)
31-40	14 (2%)
41-50	6 (1%)
51-60	3 (0%)
61-70	1 (0%)
71-80	1 (0%)
81-90	0 (0%)
91-100	1 (0%)
Total	*N* = 716 (102%)

[a]This figure, of course, means that 52 percent of the respondents admitted having committed at least one of these eight chargeable offenses during the past year. This is consistent with findings from past studies, considering the narrow time limit and the limited number and relative seriousness of offenses. These data support the view of extensive delinquent activity within the (in-school) adolescent population.

quency of delinquent behavior thus has a possible range of 0 to 160. The actual range in the sample, as shown in Table 4.8, is 0 to 96, showing that no one haphazardly marked large numbers for all offenses. Inter-item correlations yield an estimate of frequency-index reliability of .73, very much in line with earlier estimates of the reliabilities of other indexes.

The seriousness scale is based on Gold's (1966) delinquency application of Sellin and Wolfgang's (1964) scale of seriousness of offenses.

Recent analysis tends to confirm the Sellin and Wolfgang scale as additive, generalized, and useful in actually measuring the seriousness of offenses (Wellford and Wiatrowski, 1975), in spite of the reservations of some critics (Lesieur and Lehman, 1975). Small theft (less than five dollars[10]) has been excluded from the seriousness index. Likewise, car theft is excluded if it involved a friend's or a relative's car. Otherwise, the seriousness score equals the frequency score for a given offense times the seriousness weight of that offense, summed across seven offenses. Medium theft (five to fifty dollars) and medium property destruction (five to fifty dollars) are weighted one. Large theft (more than fifty dollars), large destruction (more than fifty dollars), "real" car theft, and simple assault are weighted two. And attacking someone with a weapon with a willingness to injure seriously is multiplied by a factor of three. The resulting scale has a possible range of 0 to 260, with an actual range in the sample of 0 to 113. A total of 260 students (36 percent of $N = 718$) received a nonzero seriousness-of-delinquent-behavior score.

As the reader has undoubtedly noticed, three different types of offenses have been put together in both the frequency and seriousness indexes of delinquent behavior. The presumption is that the model applies to theft, vandalism, and assault with approximately equal efficacy. These subtypes of offenses are alike in the crucial sense of being violations of legal rules. At this stage, the aim is to uncover reasons why young people violate legal norms, not specifically why one steals and another destroys. Such refined analysis will be touched upon in Chapter 6 but is to a large degree beyond the scope of this study.

Some writers have placed great emphasis on the independence of different types of offenses. Arnold (1965) reports that theft, vandalism, and assault are relatively independent and distinct types of behavior among his sample. Scott (1959) further separates theft into "general" and "interpersonal" subtypes. No one would argue against the existence of distinct dimensions of adolescent misconduct. Indeed, the finding that different adolescents do different illegal things is almost predestined, given that most of them have generally admitted only one particular type of offense. Even the present data, as reported in Table 4.7, justify the conception of theft, vandalism, and assault as separate dimensions. Although all of the delinquent behavior items load on factors other than the delinquent values dimension, they further differentiate themselves into three other factors.

Table 4.9. *Inter-index correlations (Pearson's* r*) between various indexes of delinquent behavior*

	Frequency	Seriousness	Theft	Vandalism	Assault
Assault	.54	.77	.29	.23	—
Vandalism	.58	.64	.33	—	
Theft	.93	.63	—		
Seriousness	.85	—			
Frequency	—				

For these reasons, separate measures of theft, vandalism, and assault will be retained, each being the sum of the respective items included in the frequency index. That is, theft is a four-item index with a range of zero to thirty and a reliability of .78; vandalism is a two-item, zero-to-forty index with a .81 reliability; and assault is a two-item, zero-to-forty index with a reliability of .65. The correlations between the obliquely rotated factors two, three, and four in Table 4.7 range from .24 to .37, showing substantial independence. Though the possibility of differences in the processes leading to distinct types of delinquent acts will be examined (in Chapter 6), the main analysis of the model's usefulness (in Chapter 5) will employ the overall frequency index. In addition to already stated reasons for using this index, it is noteworthy that the reliability of the overall frequency index (.73) is virtually the same as the mean of the reliabilities of the three subindexes (.75).

Finally, the correlations between pairs of measures of self-reported delinquent behavior are summarized in Table 4.9. The correlations are generally moderate to high, and all are significant beyond $p < .001$. Perhaps most salient is the strong relationship ($r = .85$) between the general frequency and seriousness measures.

At this point it may prove helpful to review briefly the theoretical constructs and their measures. Here is a summary of the indicator(s) of each concept, listed in order of their causal priority in the model:

1. *Social class.* A dichotomous variable separating underclass from earning class (UC/EC), based primarily on poverty, welfare, and unemployment. Alternative measure: a five-category father's-occupation scale (SES).
2. *Love/concern of parent for child.* A four-item index of perceptions of mother's or father's (whichever is greater) past concern and love for the respondent.

3. *Success of performance in school.* A four-item index of "real" (grades) and perceived school success.
4. *Attachment to parents.* A six-item index of the adolescent's current feelings of closeness to his or her mother or father (whichever is greater).
5. *Future-oriented perceived strain.* A realistic judgment of occupational expectations, as coded on a five-category ranking of occupations. Alternative measures: educational expectations; reported worrying about occupational future; the number of barriers perceived to make aspirations problematic; and "discrepancy scores," which take into account aspiration–expectation differences (with respect to occupations and education separately), as well as perceived barriers and worrying.
6. *Attachment to school.* A seven-item index of current feelings toward and reported involvement in school.
7. *Susceptibility to peer influence.* A single item measuring the degree of willingness to do whatever is required to please friends.
8. *Delinquent associates.* A five-item index of the reported activities and attitudes relative to delinquent behavior of the adolescent's best friends. This index incorporates items originally meant to measure anticipated peer approval for delinquency, which will no longer be considered a distinct theoretical construct.
9. *Delinquent values.* A six-item index of attitudes about the acceptability of certain illegal activities.
10. *Perceived risk of apprehension for delinquency.* A two-item index of perceived personal chances of getting caught in two hypothetical criminal situations.
11. *Delinquent behavior.* A summated index of the number of times in the past year that the adolescent reports having committed four kinds of theft, two levels of vandalism, and two degrees of assault. Alternative measures: separate theft, vandalism, and assault indexes; a seriousness scale that weights the original reported frequencies of law violation by factors representing the seriousness of each offense.

This concludes the discussion of how the variables were measured and how the data were obtained. The remaining chapters deal with the "fit" between the model and the data.

5. Analyzing the results

The primary method of checking the tenability of the causal model will involve what is commonly known as path analysis. It entails solving for the parameters of the set of structural equations that are implied by the model (Figure 5.1).

The general sense of a test of a path model is briefly described in the early portions of Chapter 3. Here it should merely be restated that path analysis is not a means of demonstrating causality. The analysis must assume a priori that there is a particular causal ordering and that the system is causally closed to unknown influences on the covariations present. This "specification" of the model can never be proven correct.

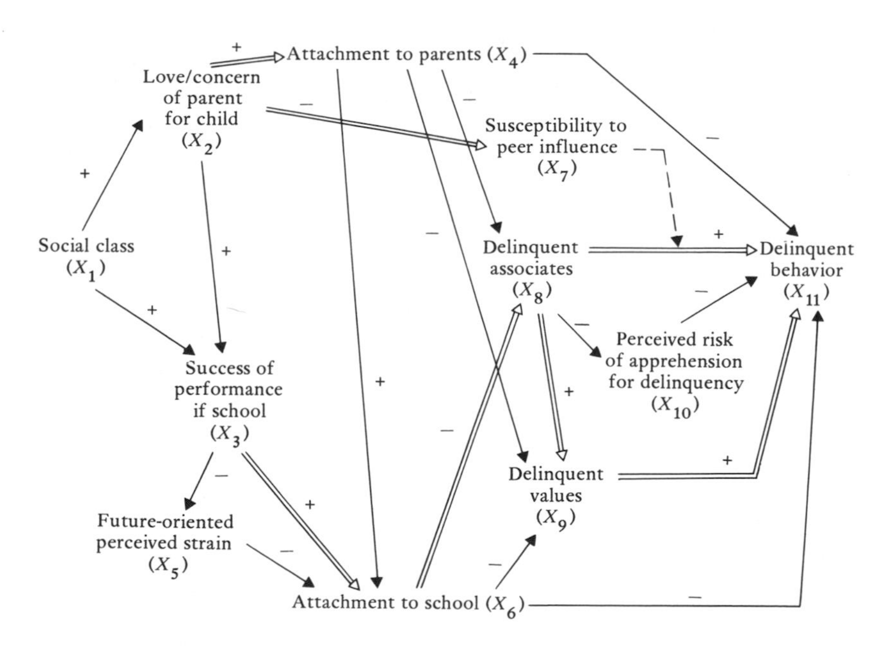

Figure 5.1. The complete testable model

Nor can it be derived from the coefficients. But specific regression or path coefficients inconsistent with the reasoning may provide clues to improper specifications. However, inconsistent results could also be caused by sampling variability, measurement errors, and/or real structural differences. The reader must recognize the difference between what is assumed and what is demonstrated and also be aware of the numerous factors other than causal laws that can influence the estimates of the structural parameters.

By assuming one-way causation (a recursive model), the system of equations becomes solvable, in that the knowns outnumber the unknowns. Through multiple regression techniques, the regression of each variable in the model on every other *prior* variable will be determined. It is anticipated that we will be unable to reject the null hypothesis of a zero coefficient in each case of a "missing arrow" in Figure 5.1. Paths will be retained (i.e., an inferred effect "verified") on the joint bases of the statistical significance and the magnitudes of regression coefficients, depending on the specific analysis and sample size involved.

The regression coefficients will be substantively interpreted as slopes, that is, the amount of change in the dependent variable given a unit change in the appropriate independent variable, controlling for other relevant independent variables. In general, both unstandardized regression coefficients and standardized regression ("path") coefficients will be reported.[1]

In addition to the assumptions of correct specification of causal ordering, causal closure (or uncorrelated error terms), and recursiveness, path analysis entails the usual assumptions of multiple regression.[2]

It has already been shown that the reliabilities of many of the measures are less than perfect. Thus parameter estimates will generally be attenuated, as measurement error in an independent variable (X) reduces the magnitude of the estimate (b_{yx}) relative to the true population parameter (β_{yx}). There are other possible distortions in the causal inferences that could result from imperfect measurement. In particular, controls for imperfectly measured variables do not totally eradicate indirect effects through these variables. Furthermore, some relationships could be inflated when controls are imperfect. But attenuation is the most common result. Consequently, later estimates of explained variance should generally be conservative. But the primary task at hand is to test for the existence of, and the *relative* magnitudes of, selected causal processes, rather than to explain a certain proportion of variance. As Schuessler (1971) points out, the validity of a path model is not dependent upon its predictive efficacy (R^2).

Except for measurement and specification errors (the latter, it is to be hoped, having been minimized throughout Chapter 3), regression analysis appears to be quite robust (Bohrnstedt and Carter, 1971). That is, results tend to be sufficiently accurate in spite of violations of the other assumptions.[3] Given the robustness of the parametric procedures, the power to be gained from parametric statistics seems to offset the risk of violating assumptions, despite the highly technical criticisms of some writers (cf. Wilson, 1970). As Kim (1975:294) states, the "parametric strategy is more compatible with the successive refinement of our measurement and theories and with the interplay between substantive theory and measurement." And finally, though path analysis is not robust as far as multicollinearity is concerned, a concerted effort has been made to guard against that phenomenon (one theoretical construct was eliminated in so doing) through careful composition of the indicators utilizing factor analysis.

Because there are alternative measures for the concepts *social class, strain,* and *delinquent behavior,* there will be several solutions to the set of multiple regression equations implied by the model. For each solution (referred to as computer run) the combination of indicators involved, as well as the sample size, will be reported. The variation in sample size is caused by variable nonresponse rates to questionnaire items.[4]

The results of the initial run are pictured in Figure 5.2. Underclass versus earning class is used as the measure of *social class;* occupational expectations are utilized to measure *strain;* and the combined frequency scale is the indicator of *delinquent behavior.* This initial run will serve as a reference point for substantive interpretations as well as for later comparisons incorporating alternative indexes. For each path, the standardized path coefficient[5] is written just above or preceding the corresponding unstandardized regression coefficient (which is in parentheses). All (and only) paths with coefficents significant beyond $p < .01$ (restrictive because of the large sample) are included in Figure 5.2.[6] Error terms are omitted for pictorial clarity. The discussion of the substantive implications of these results will follow according to the causal ordering of the variables.

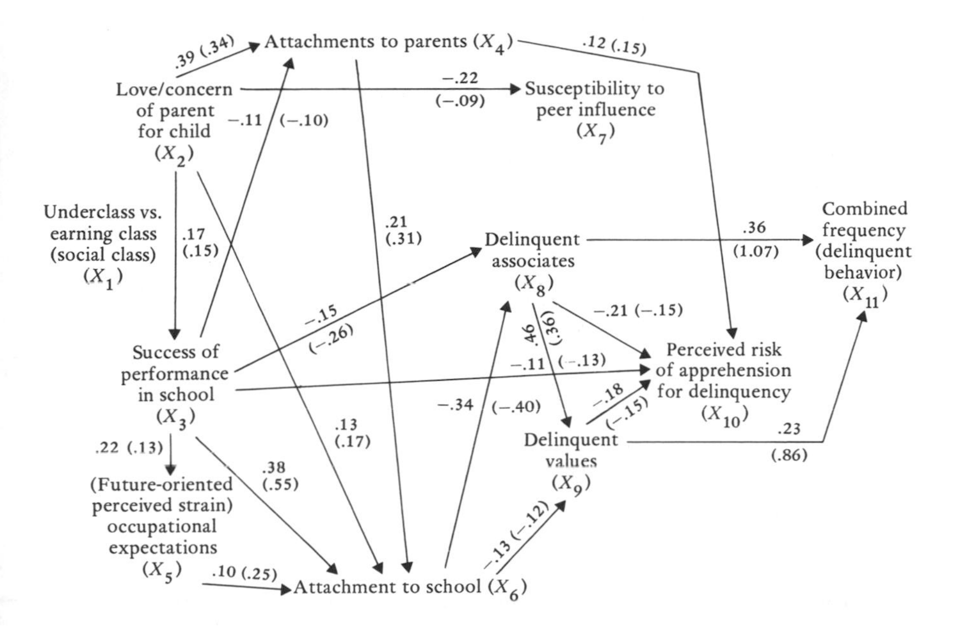

Figure 5.2. Results for the total sample ($N = 549$), including all paths with coëfficients significant beyond $p < .01$, employing the following measures: underclass vs. earning class (X_1), occupational expectations (X_5), combined frequency (X_{11}). ($R^2 = .27$)

Social class

The data simply do not support the contention that class is a salient factor in generating delinquent involvement. Even measured as a dichotomous "dummy variable" separating underclass from earning class, social class has no statistically significant effect on any other variable in the model. The greatest nonsignificant effect of social class in the initial run (not shown in Figure 5.2) is a path coefficient of .08 ($p < .05$) to parental love. That is, there is a shadow of evidence that if being underclass affects anything, the model is correct in predicting a lower level of parental love. But the fact remains that very little evidence for any effect of social class is found in the data.

But could this apparent refutation of the relevance of social class be caused in part by research methods? How do these results compare with results using a more traditional father's-occupation measure of social class? To gain insight into this question, a run was conducted with only one change from the run that produced Figure 5.2 – SES by father's occupation became the new measure of social class.

The only change was that SES (as opposed to UC/EC) produced a slight, significant effect from class to school success. As Hirschi (1969) and many others have found with similar measures, social class is not shown to be of great causal efficacy. However, it appears that the offspring of professionals, executives, and other (better-educated) white-collar employees perform slightly better in school. Perhaps the UC/ES measure of class fails to recognize important distinctions within the earning class – especially concerning education. Certainly it would not be difficult to devise a trichotomous class measure, for example, separating underclass, blue collar, and white collar. On the other hand, the significant effect is quite small in magnitude ($p = .15$), which argues against devoting much more effort to the search for a social class effect on delinquent behavior.

Yet it remains disturbing in light of the discussion in Chapter 2 that SES "does something" and UC/EC does not. The opposite outcome was expected. Perhaps the answer lies in the relative lack of variation along the UC/EC measure as applied to the present sample. Lack of variation in an independent variable attenuates its apparent effects on other variables and decreases the reliability of estimates. And there are only 58 of 734 respondents categorized as underclass (zero) on the UC/EC dummy variable. Schoenberg (1975:70) reports similar inadequacies in variation in related measures. Perhaps if a study encompassed a ghetto area, thereby providing greater variation by class, then class might yet prove to be an influence. So although there is no evidence of class effects, neither is there conclusive evidence of a total lack of class effects. But as stated in Chapter 3, other data seem to suggest that even the UC/EC conceptualization is unlikely to show very great causal influence (Berger and Simon, 1974).

Love/concern of parent for child

As stated in Chapter 3, the central prediction regarding parental love is not that it is influenced by social class, but rather that it leads to attachment to parents and reduces susceptibility to peer influence. Parental love should also (to a lesser degree) increase the chances for school success (see Figure 5.1 for predictions). The data are consistent with the model. Figure 5.2 shows that children to a relatively high degree[7] do seem more likely to attach themselves to parents who show them greater love and respect, that is, to parents from whom they have derived greater amounts of self-esteem. Support for this reasoning is added by the effect of parental love on susceptibility to peer influence shown in Figure 5.2. Greater parental love (as perceived and reported by the child) apparently decreases an adolescent's desire for peer approval.

It is particularly significant that this effect of perceived parental love exists after controlling for parental attachment. This effect highlights the theoretical importance of distinguishing between these two dimensions of parent–child interaction in the search for causal processes. It is also interesting that parental love is the *only* influence (of X_1 through X_6 as possible causes) on susceptibility to peer influence.[8] Thus these findings may have pinpointed a very specific causal mechanism that certainly deserves future empirical and theoretical attention.

Finally, the data confirm the hypothesis of a mild but significant direct effect of parental love on success in school. Likewise, there is a mild effect of parental love on school attachment, which was not predicted. Perhaps children "reciprocate" a parent's love directly by attaching themselves to the parent-approved institution of the school. But the effect is too minor to suggest important unforeseen processes.

Success of performance in school

The testable model (Figure 5.1) predicts that school success influences delinquent behavior primarily through affecting attachment to school – largely directly but also through future-oriented perceived strain. School success is also expected to lessen the degree of desire for peer approval and therefore decrease susceptibility to peer influence.

The data support the proposition that school success is a major contributor to the strength of an adolescent's linkage to the school (see Figure 5.2). It is one of the highest path coefficients in the entire run.

But school success does not seem to affect certain other variables in expected ways. There is no significant path from school success to susceptibility to peer influence. Evidently, past successes in school (primarily academic) are not valued enough in the peer social world to provide a satisfactory "rep" or identity that insulates the person from desires to gain peer acceptance at any cost. The persistence of willingness to do things to gain peer acceptance, regardless of the level of academic success, implies that academic achievement is but one isolated dimension of adolescent status striving. The adolescent does not succeed with peers simply because of classroom achievement. This, of course, is consistent with the common observation that "brains" or "eggheads" are often derogated by less-capable peers.

Perhaps more theoretically significant is the relatively weak influence from school success to futuristic strain, for a great body of literature has built up around the issue of strain. The data indicate that the relevance of past educational achievement to perceptions of future occupational success or failures may not be as great as is often supposed. This issue of the role of strain will be discussed in more detail later in this chapter.

Finally, school success has unpredicted significant (yet weak) inferred effects on parental attachment, delinquent associates, and perceived risk of apprehension. All seem explainable after the fact, but it must be admitted that almost any finding imaginable can be explained once it exists.

It makes sense that greater school success leads to fewer delinquent associates. The error in the model was simply in stressing the indirect path through school attachment while ignoring the direct path. This is but one indication of what appears to be a general underestimation in the theorizing of the direct importance of school success (and delinquent associates) in the overall causal scheme.

In the theory (Figure 5.1), school success has a positive but indirect effect on perceived risk of apprehension. That is, school success leads to school attachment, which decreases delinquent associates, thereby increasing perceived risk. Although that causal chain is verified, school success also has a direct *inverse* effect on perceived risk, which, according to the model, should increase the likelihood of delinquent behavior. A discussion of the effects of perceived risk will be presented later, but here it seems that delinquent behavior appears to be less risky to those who do well in school. One interpretation is that these students are smarter and therefore able to make more accurate judgments about their actual chances of getting caught. Because actual risks are very low, the perceptions of low risk by school achievers can be interpreted as "quite accurate" rather than as "free from deterring fears." After all, these same school achievers do have greater stakes in conformity through school attachment than do lesser achievers, and they have fewer delinquent associates. Nevertheless, the total direct and indirect effects in Figure 5.2 from school success to perceived risk are slightly negative.

Some of that curious negative effect of school success on perceived risk is through parent attachment. The unexpected component is the negative path from school success to parent attachment – two supposedly delinquency-preventing variables. It is a very minor (barely significant) effect, to be sure, but it exists just the same. Apparently this effect represents the process Hewitt (1970:68) describes, wherein school failure can cause the adolescent to turn to parents as well as peers for the missing self-esteem. Thus parents may get a second chance at providing self-esteem for their offspring. In light of the absence of school-success effects on susceptibility to peer influence, it seems that increased attachment to parents may be a more common result of difficulties in school than is increasing the quest for peer acceptance.

Attachment to parents

As described in their respective sections of this chapter, parental love and school success affect attachment to parents. Parental love has the expected strong positive effect and school success has a surprising but weak negative influence.

In theory, parent attachment is given a central place as a determinant of a delinquency-controlling stake in conformity. Yet the results shown in Figure 5.2 do not support those contentions. There are virtually no direct effects from parent attachment to delinquent behavior ($p = .003$, not shown in Figure 5.2 because of nonsignificance), to delinquent associates ($p = -.062$), or to delinquent values ($p = -.014$). The only predicted effect verified by the data is the positive influence of parent attachment on school attachment ($p = .21$). Finally, there is an unpredicted but interpretable weak positive effect on perceived risk. It seems plausible that adolescents more attached to their parents are more likely to believe conventional maxims that parents tend to espouse, including crime doesn't pay, in spite of (or in ignorance of) contradictory evidence.

The apparent lack of causal efficacy of parent attachment is troublesome to the theory. Either the theory or the methods of testing (or both) need some revision. It might be useful first to examine some possible methodological explanations for these surprising results.

One primary concern is with the relatively high degree of correlation between parental love and parent attachment. As Gordon (1968) points

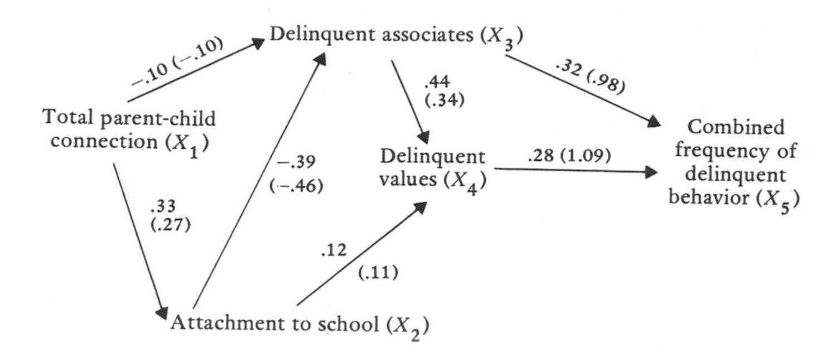

Figure 5.3. Results for the total sample ($N = 676$) with the effects of the "total parent–child connection" in a simplified model, including all paths with coefficients significant beyond $p < .01$. ($R^2 = .27$)

out, correlations among independent variables can produce misleading results concerning the effects of each independent variable on a dependent variable. That is, if parental love and parent attachment are "redundant," then "true" effects of parent attachment may be tipped in favor of parental love. Or, if the two parent variables are more repetitive than other independent variables, the effects of parents in general on associates, values, and so forth will be divided up and will appear relatively trivial.

Consequently, a more general indicator of parent–child relationships has been developed to determine if its use implies greater causal efficacy for parental ties. The composite measure is the simple sum of scores of the parental-love and parent-attachment indexes, to which is added the adolescent's score on caring what parents think (see the Appendix). This last component is included because of its intuitive appeal (face validity) as a measure of parent-induced stake in conformity, even though it was excluded from the attachment index on the basis of factor analysis.

The effects of this total parent–child connection on the major subsequent variables are summarized in Figure 5.3. The impact on school attachment turns out to be almost identical to the sum of the effects of parental love and attachment on that variable in Figure 5.2. And there are still no direct effects of parent–child connections on delinquent values or behavior, with only a small, marginally significant influence on delinquent associates.

In short, there is only slim evidence of a causal role for affective ties to parents in generating delinquent behavior.[9] That role seems to be through influencing the degree of the child's attachment to school. Perhaps attachment or control theories have overstated the salience of an adolescent's ties to his or her parents. Indeed, Schoenberg (1975:78–82) also finds affective ties to parents to be of virtually no direct effect on delinquent behavior and to influence delinquent associations merely moderately in only some of his subsamples.

Future-oriented perceived strain

The data (Figure 5.2) exclude strain from all but a minor role in producing delinquent behavior. Perceptions of lower occupational expectations tend to follow a lack of school success, but those perceptions in turn have an extremely slight effect on the strength of present ties to the school. Once again, either the theory or the methods need some revision. As described in Chapters 2 and 3, I predict that futuristic frustrations are simply not very relevant to an adolescent's degree or likelihood of involvement in illegal acts. But in deference to the great body of strain literature, and in search of greater insights, various measurements have been developed for the strain construct. Perhaps an alternative measure of strain (specified in the Appendix) will appear relevant to delinquent behavior. There are five such measures in addition to simple occupational expectations.

A rather complex discrepancy score – based upon differences between occupational aspirations and expectations – was discussed in Chapter 4 as an indicator of strain. Moreover, it includes items that rule out respondents who report a difference in aspirations and expectations but who do not seem frustrated by that difference.

The results of the run with this "purified" discrepancy score as the measure of strain are summarized in Figure 5.4. These results, compared to Figure 5.2,[10] confirm the suspicion that expectations alone are a more salient feature of futuristic perceptions than are more vague and complicated discrepancy measures. There is literally no role whatsoever for this revised measure of strain in producing self-reported delinquent behavior. It is not influenced by school success (or social class), nor does it affect school attachment (or anything else). However, there may yet be some role for futuristic strain within the context of school experiences, as evidenced when occupational expectations alone were used to measure strain. Yet it is difficult to understate the case for

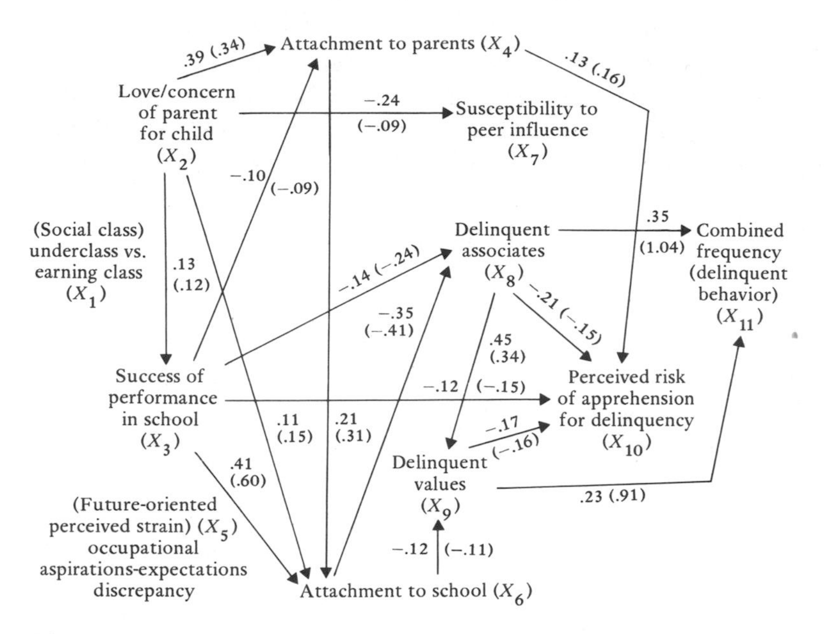

Figure 5.4. Results for the total sample ($N = 616$), including all paths with coefficients significant beyond $p < .01$, employing the following measures: underclass vs. earning class (X_1), occupational discrepancy (X_5), combined frequency (X_{11}). ($R^2 = .26$)

strain. Schoenberg (1975:70–1), for example, does not even include discrepancies or expectations in his causal models because of negligible total correlations of these variables with delinquent behavior.

It is not necessary to rediagram the entire causal model to examine the effects of employing the other measures of strain, for all of the non-strain processes remain stable. Upon examining these other results, it appears that *if indeed futuristic strain does play a role,* educational expectations are a good indicator of strain, but worry, educational discrepancy, and perceived barriers are not. The data indicate that school success significantly influences educational expectations ($p = .37$), which in turn affect school attachment ($p = .19$). Educational expectations also have a direct effect on delinquent associates ($p = -.11$). In fact, the predicted effects of strain are somewhat greater if educational rather than occupational expectations are utilized. However, the occupational measure will remain as the central indicator in this study, because strain theories emphasize legitimate job opportunities and because that indicator entails less redundancy or repetitiveness with the other school-related variables.

The reported degree of worrying about future jobs has opposite effects from those expected. Greater worry (strain?) leads to *greater* attachment to school ($p = .16$). It seems that worrying signifies conscientiousness rather than frustration. As an apparently invalid indicator of strain (assuming occupational and educational expectations to be valid), worry's inclusion in the occupational-discrepancy index probably accounts for some of that index's failure to have effects. Interestingly, worry is not significantly influenced by school performance, but it is affected by parental love ($p = -.11$) and parent attachment ($p = .22$). Evidently, being treated as important by parents gives a child confidence and thereby reduces worry; being attached to parents seems to make it more important to the child to meet parental expectations and thereby increases worry.

The number of perceived barriers to job and education goals does not seem very useful as a separate indicator of strain. It, too, is influenced by parental love ($p = .14$), but it has no significant (beyond $p < .01$) effects on any other variable. Thus another perhaps invalid indicator of strain is also a component of the indexes of occupational and educational discrepancies.

It is no surprise, therefore, that the index of educational-aspirations–expectations discrepancy fares no better in showing strain effects. It influences nothing in the model. But it does seem to be slightly influenced by the variable underclass versus earning class ($p = -.13$). Though this effect is minor, it adds a bit to earlier-stated reservations about denying a role for class (UC/EC) on the basis of the present sample, which includes only a small portion of underclass adolescents.

It has been shown that occupational and educational expectations affect school attachment (and therefore delinquent behavior, which has yet to be discussed) in a manner consistent with the theoretical model. But it was also noted in Chapter 2 that expectations alone are valid indicators of both social bonds and strain. Which process underlies these factors? A look at some key partial correlations may clarify the issue of the tenability of certain control theory versus strain theory implications. The partial correlation between occupational aspirations (*OA*) and delinquent behavior (*DB*), controlling for occupational expectations (*OE*), allows for a so-called crucial test. For the total sample,

$r_{DB,OA \cdot OE} = -.16$. This means that given all students with equal expectations, greater aspirations "control" delinquency, which conclusion supports Hirschi's (1969) control formulation. But it also means that students with greater aspiration–expectation discrepancies (a rise in aspirations with expectations controlled) – those with greater strain – are *less* involved in delinquent behavior. If the difference between desires and expectations were the relevant factor, and if aspirations alone were not a control against deviance, $r_{DB,OA \cdot OE}$ should be positive. The same general finding occurs with educational aspirations (EA) and expectations (EE): $r_{DB,EA \cdot EE} = -.04$.

On the other hand, $r_{DB,OE \cdot OA}$ and $r_{DB,EE \cdot EA}$ should be negative according to both strain and control reasoning. Given an aspiration level, those with greater expectations (a control against deviance) also have higher expectations in relation to aspirations (less strain). In fact, $r_{DB,OE \cdot OA} = -.04$ and $r_{DB,EE \cdot EA} = -.10$. It appears that strain and bonds acting together do no better than bonds acting in spite of strain.

The most reasonable conclusion – based on these findings as well as the lack of effects of the other measures of strain – is that the small observed expectations effects are probably not caused by underlying frustrations arising from perceptions of limited opportunities. Expectations (and aspirations) are better viewed as indicators of current "commitment to conventional action" (Hirschi, 1969:chap. 9). Thus "future-oriented perceived strain" should perhaps be replaced in the theoretical model (Figure 5.1) by "commitment to conventional action" or "commitment to career and educational success." It is highly plausible that such a commitment is indeed influenced by past school success and in turn affects present school attachment. At any rate, the data fail to provide support for the strain theory formulations incorporated in the model.

Attachment to school

The effects of parental love, parent attachment, occupational expectations, and school performance on school attachment have already been discussed. None is inconsistent with the formulation.

Furthermore, the effects of school attachment on subsequent variables are largely in accord with the theoretical reasoning. The greatest result of higher school attachment is the lowering of delinquent associates; moreover, school attachment has the single greatest effect on delinquent associates. These findings support the conception of the school as the central arena for the sifting and sorting of adolescent companionships, which prove to be so relevant to delinquent behavior. To the extent that birds of a feather flock together, the level of attachment to school seems to be the central delinquency-relevant "feathering" criterion.

Although school attachment fails to affect delinquent behavior *directly* in a significant way ($p = -.01$), it does influence law violations not only through delinquent associates but also through delinquent values, as predicted. The lack of a predicted direct effect is most likely an indication of the theoretical underestimation of the role of delinquent associates in relation to attachments per se.

Susceptibility to peer influence

From Figure 5.2 it appears that susceptibility to peer influence is affected by parental love, but that it in turn affects nothing. As a direct causal variable, in fact, susceptibility to peer influence fails to show significant ($p < .01$) effects on X_8 through X_{11}. But there were no predictions in the formulation (Figure 5.1) that it would have any such independent effects.

The theory predicts only that there is a significant interaction between susceptibility to peer influence and delinquent associates concerning the latter's effects on delinquent behavior. That is, having delinquent associates should become more predictive of misdeeds if the adolescent feels a stronger need for their approval and is therefore more easily influenced by them. Interactions can be incorporated into a set of equations corresponding to a causal model by use of a product term.[11] In this model, the new interaction variable would be (X_7X_8), and it would be predicted to have direct effects on delinquent behavior. However, it would be necessary to test simultaneously for separate effects of delinquent associates (X_8), as it is predicted that delinquent friends will affect deviance in spite of a reported lack of susceptibility to peer influence. That is, it would be incorrect to give a zero score on a multiplicative "delinquent associates and susceptibility to their influence" variable as the only indicator of peer group environment, because a deviant peer group environment may affect delinquency involvement even among those reporting zero willingness to do things in order to please friends.

To include the product term (X_7X_8) in the same equation as X_8 alone, however, may cause difficulties in interpretation because of multicollinearity. The product term is a function of the components, and the correlation between delinquent associates and the product term is $r = .86$. It would be extremely difficult to separate the effects and relative importance of these variables in delinquency causation. Moreover, sampling errors could yield misleading parameter estimates. In short, the product term will not be entered in *general* regression solutions.

It is still possible, however, to gain insight into the tenability of interaction effects by conducting a separate regression analysis, providing that the problem of multicollinearity is not so fatal as to render it impossible to disentangle interaction from separate additive effects. When susceptibility to peer influence (X_7), delinquent associates (X_8), and the multiplicative interaction term (X_7X_8) are simultaneously included as independent variables in a regression equation for delinquent behavior, the greatest effect is from the interaction term ($p = .33$, $p < .001$), less effect is shown by delinquent associates alone ($p = .19$, $p < .03$), and virtually no additive influence comes from susceptibility to peer influence ($p = .05$, $p < .30$). These results coincide with the theory.

Additionally, regressing delinquent behavior on delinquent associates alone ($p = .47$, $p < .001$) and then on delinquent associates and the interaction product together shows that the interaction term explains only an additional 2 percent (from 22 percent to 24 percent) of the total variation in delinquent behavior. Omitting an interactive term from the general regression solutions, therefore, does not lead to a substantial understatement of the overall role of peers. But that does not mean that the interaction is theoretically unimportant, for the category delinquent associates also adds very little explained variance (2 percent) if the product term ($p = .47$, $p < .001$) is included first.

Finally, the effects of delinquent associates on delinquent behavior were checked for subsamples of high and low susceptibility to peer influence. The results show greater effects among the highly susceptible group ($N = 293$, $p = .54$, $b = 1.87$, $p < .01$) than among those less susceptible ($N = 419$, $p = .39$, $b = 1.03$, $p < .01$), findings which are consistent with the theoretical predictions.

Substantively, it appears that the model is tenable on the influence of susceptibility to peer influence. Such susceptibility does seem to have a conditioning effect that increases the likelihood of deviance in some adolescents. But it is impossible to place relative quantification on such effects. It can merely be asserted that parental love (as the precursor to susceptibility to peer influence) has even more effect on delinquent behavior than is shown by tracing the paths in Figure 5.2.

Delinquent associates

The data indicate (see Figure 5.2 or Figure 5.4) that school-related factors have the greatest direct influence on the type of friends (delinquent or nondelinquent) an adolescent has. Somewhat surprisingly, parent attachment has only a minor indirect effect through school attachment.

As to the inferred effects of delinquent associates, they appear to be most clearly substantiated of all delinquency predictors considered here. As Schoenberg (1975) finds in three distinct data sets, the present data support the proposition that delinquent associates play a central role in the causation of illegal behavior. As the model predicts, a substantial amount of the influence of delinquent friends on delinquent behavior rests in a direct causal linkage – the strongest path to illegalities in the model.

Moreover, peer associates seem to influence perceptions of the acceptability of certain illegal activities, as these associates have a strong influence on delinquent values. Finally, delinquent associates have the predicted influence on perceptions of the risks involved in committing certain crimes. Having had more exposure to delinquent friends decreases the perceived certainty of getting caught.

Delinquent values

It has been previously discussed how attachment to school and delinquent associates have the predicted effects on delinquent values. Once again the theory seemingly overestimated the role of attachment to parents, as it has no significant direct influence on delinquent values.

The adolescent's values concerning delinquent behavior in turn influence the likelihood that he or she will commit illegal acts. Delinquent values have the predicted positive effect on frequency of delinquent behavior.

Once again there is an unexpected (inverse) effect on perceived risk of apprehension. Perhaps those seeing an act as more acceptable do so in part because they perceive it as more common, regardless of the amount of delinquent activities of their best friends. A natural correlate of such an "everybody's doing it, so it must be okay" attitude would be a perception that "they all get away with it" (because in actuality most of them do). So acceptability becomes a forerunner to perceptions of low risk.

Perceived risk of apprehension for delinquency

Throughout the discussion of the variables in this theory, it has been noted that several of those variables show a causal effect on perceived risk of apprehension (see Figure 5.2 or Figure 5.4). School success seems to have positive and negative influences; greater attachments to parents seem to increase the likelihood of deterrence; and more delinquent friends and values lessen the perceived certainty of getting caught.

Unfortunately for the theory, the process appears to end at perceived risk. There is only a very slight indication of the predicted inverse effect (which fails to meet the significance criterion for Figure 5.2 and is therefore not shown). That is, the path coefficient on the route from perceived certainty to delinquent behavior is −.06. But, of course, making much ado about coefficients of such small magnitude could simply be a case of jumping to conclusions based on chance variations.

Yet finding several variables that have small but significant effects on perceived certainty is a contribution toward the understanding of that only recently investigated phenomenon. Moreover, there is no solid empirical reason from the present data to deny Tittle and Rowe's (1974: 459) assertion that certainty of punishment does deter, "but that this influence does not show noticeable results until certainty has reached at least moderate levels." Perhaps perceived risk of apprehension for delinquency would deter otherwise uncontrolled adolescents if law enforcement were substantially more efficient and adolescents knew it.

On the other hand, the results show that positive motivation from delinquent friends may have a substantial effect on the law violations of an adolescent, increasing his or her illegal behavior above a level that might be caused simply by relative freedom from conventional attachments. This peer group motivation (to show daring, to gain "rep") may increase the "pleasure" of deviating in a given situation to such an extent that the amount of "pain" (certainty) needed to deter would have to be unreasonably high. Furthermore, although actual certainty of apprehension for the situations studied (questionnaire items 101 and 102; see the Appendix) is undoubtedly below Tittle and Rowe's (1974) moderate level necessary to deter, the students' reported perceptions of

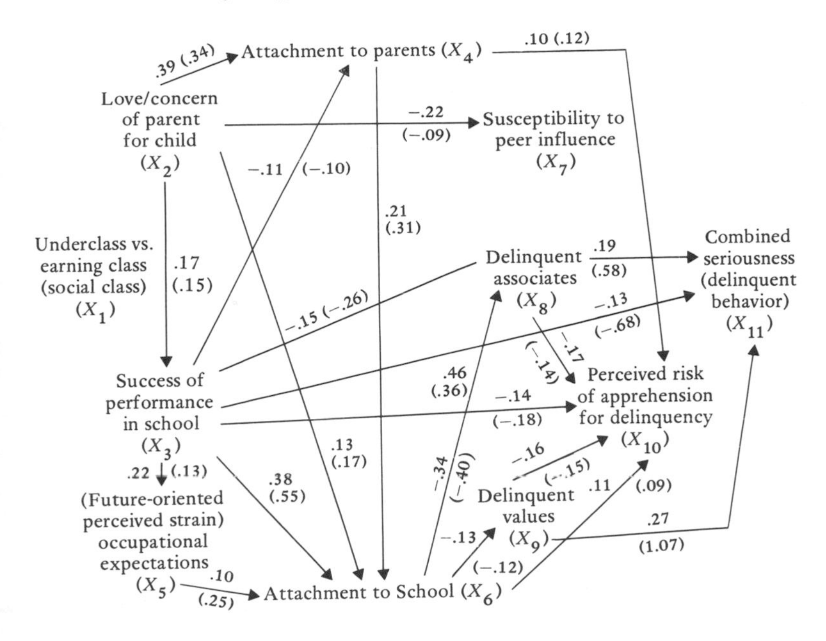

Figure 5.5. Results for the total sample (N = 549), including all paths with coefficients significant beyond $p < .01$, employing the following measures: underclass vs. earning class (X_1), occupational expectations (X_5), combined seriousness (X_{11}). ($R^2 = .21$)

certainty are surprisingly high. For shoplifting, 58 percent see their chances of getting caught as 50 percent or more, whereas exactly half see the same risk in school burglary. These perceptions seem to be above a moderate level, and deterrence still fails to occur to a significant degree. Apparently, either actual certainty must be tremendously increased for the threat of apprehension to deter, or delinquent acts are quite immune to deterrence because of their situational, peer-oriented nature. In some cases, for example, greater risk is probably even an incentive to commit an act, in order to show daring, during these formative years.

Delinquent behavior

Before summing up the findings among the total sample, it would be wise to make sure that the results would not differ dramatically if the analysis had used a seriousness rather than a frequency index of illegal acts. Figure 5.5 summarizes the results of a run identical to that pictured in Figure 5.2 except for the delinquent behavior measure. Most path coefficients are nearly identical. For one thing, eliminating the more trivial offenses does not give rise to a social class difference, as some would imply it should (see Chapter 2). The two major differences are (*a*) the emergence of a direct effect of school performance on delinquent behavior not present in Figure 5.2 and (*b*) an apparent shifting in Figure 5.5 of some of the direct causal effect of delinquent associates toward indirect effects through delinquent values.[12]

The first difference is really no difference at all. It results from the always arbitrary setting of a level of significance necessary for inclusion in the diagrams. In the frequency run, the path coefficient from school performance to delinquent behavior (not shown in Figure 5.2) is −.09 (just missing significance). This coefficient hardly differs from the seriousness run's $p = -.11$ ($p < .009$). School performance has a slight direct inverse effect on both the frequency and the seriousness of delinquent behavior.

The greater salience of delinquent values, relative to delinquent associates, for seriousness of illegalities is probably partly real and partly artifactual. The items comprising the index of delinquent values (see the Appendix) are weighted slightly more toward assault and vandalism than toward theft, whereas the frequency index is more highly related to theft and the seriousness measure is more correlated with assault and vandalism (as reported in Table 4.9). In other words, if more of the values items had dealt with theft, the effect of delinquent values on that more-highly-related-to-theft frequency index (Figure 5.2) might have appeared to be as large as it is on the seriousness index (Figure 5.5).

Future research could examine the relative effects of associates and values on the commission of specific offenses, tapping values relative to the particular act in question. I feel that the pattern shown in these data will remain, that is, that personal values acquire more salience in decisions to commit or abstain from more serious offenses. It is not difficult to be talked into or to drift into the common, relatively minor offenses that contribute greatly to a frequency score. Values related to the offenses in question may not even vary significantly, given an infracultural view of extensive acceptance of situational deviation. When values do not vary, they cannot cause. And lesser variation attenuates apparent effects.

It requires greater soul-searching to decide whether to commit a more serious offense (such as assault). There is probably more variation in the degree to which (the range of situations in which) adolescents view it as acceptable. Hence, personal values take on a greater role in predicting a measure that has given greater weight to more serious offenses.

Although this is a significant finding in and of itself, the differences in the causes of frequency and seriousness are not so great as to preclude a single general interpretation of the findings. Figures 5.2 and 5.5 both point to delinquent associates as a key variable in generating delinquent behavior and influencing delinquent values, which in turn have a separate impact on law violation.

The relative importance of the variables

The most likely candidates for "specification change" (in the form of elimination from the model) are futuristic strain, social class, and perceived risk of apprehension. Class and perceived risk do nothing, and strain is probably more accurately conceptualized, in the etiology of delinquent behavior, as lack of commitment to conventional work and education patterns. Such commitment logically falls into the same causal ordering as the original strain, or it could be subsumed into a broader measure of attachment to school. Of all the variables in the formulation, there appear to be the fewest good reasons for reservations about the elimination of futuristic strain or frustration from the vocabulary of delinquency causation.

Social class likewise has virtually no explanatory value for the present sample, no matter how it is measured. However, there is reason to believe that the underclass/earning-class conceptualization may not have received a fair test herein. Its use may yet show that class does influence delinquent behavior (probably slightly) in areas with substantial underclass membership. But SES of father's occupation will probably never prove useful, and the present findings join a long list of others that have refuted its supposed relevance. Perceived risk of getting caught, on the other hand, could deserve its theorized place in the causal scheme for certain offenses and situations characterized by high certainty of punishment. It definitely appears to be influenced in reasonable ways by prior variables in the model. But in the general scheme of delinquent behavior causation, it appears that deterrence does not operate to a significant degree.

It appears that the original theoretical formulation overemphasized the importance of school attachment and especially of parent attachment, while understating the relevance of school performance, delinquent values, and especially delinquent associates. Perceived parental love acts much as expected, and its extra effects on delinquent behavior, through susceptibility to peer influence, are a fertile ground for future inquiry – especially as peers seem to play such a central role.

A stake-in-conformity explanation of delinquency based on parent and school ties seems to suffer as a result of the findings. To be sure, the best explanation incorporates both these control variables and the differential-association (with peers and with values or definitions) variables, but the data point to the latter for greatest influence. Schoenberg (1975) reaches similar conclusions and also similarly finds that, within the cluster of controls, it is the school factors that appear to be most relevant. It seems that an adolescent's public life has as much or more to do with his or her deviance or conformity than do "under-the-roof" experiences. Furthermore, the extent of law violation by friends seems to be the key element in the youth's public life. And it is affected only slightly and indirectly by parent–child relationships in the present sample. The primary determinants of delinquent associates are school attachment and school performance, the latter having more direct influence than anticipated.

A ranking of the total standardized direct and indirect effects of the variables on delinquent behavior (from Figure 5.2[13]) is presented in Table 5.1. It represents the effects of the variables that can be inferred if the assumed causal model is actually correct and summarizes the findings to a certain extent. It also indicates that 27 percent of the variation in frequency of delinquent behavior is explained by significant paths ($p < .01$). With 73 percent of the variation left unexplained, it should be admitted that none of the major theories appear to be doing very well. Relatively speaking, however, delinquent associates appear to be of primary importance, followed by delinquent values. Next come the school factors, followed by the parent variables. Last are strain, perceived risk, and social class. These conclusions, of course, are subject to the assumption of correct model specification and to cautions about imperfect measures that have not been corrected for attenuation.

Because these results imply a differential-association view at the expense of an attachment or stake-in-conformity explanation, further exploration into the role of delinquent associates seems profitable. Indeed, locating the place of delinquent associates in the complex etiology of delinquent behavior is perhaps the most basic and most discussed issue in the literature. It has recently received the careful attention of Friday

Table 5.1. *Rank order of the total causal effects of variables* X_1 *through* X_{10} *on delinquent behavior* (X_{11}) *from Figure 5.2, standardized coefficients* ($R^2 = .27$)

Independent variable	Total causal effects	Direct causal effects	Indirect causal effects
Delinquent associates	.40	.30	.10
Delinquent values	.20	.20	.00
Attachment to school	-.14	.00	-.14
School performance	-.11	.00	-.11
Parental love	-.05[a]	.00	-.05
Attachment to parents	-.03	.00	-.03
Occupational expectations	-.01	.00	-.01
Susceptibility to peer influence	.00[a]	.00	.00
Perceived risk of apprehension	.00	.00	.00
Underclass/earning class	.00	.00	.00

[a]Plus some extra interaction effect through susceptibility to peer influence.

and Hage (1976), Empey and Lubeck (1971*a* and 1971*b*), Jensen (1972), Hepburn (1976), and Schoenberg (1975).

Are peers a motivating force in law violation in addition to (or in spite of) the adolescent's level of social-bond constraints? Or is having delinquent friends, along with holding delinquent values and committing delinquent acts, largely just another result of freedom from social attachments? In short, are delinquent associates active or passive participants in the causal scheme? Of the above-mentioned researchers, Jensen (1972) and Hepburn (1976) conclude basically that both models are correct. Schoenberg (1975) seems to emphasize an active role for peers, whereas Friday and Hage (1976) and Empey and Lubeck (1971*a* and 1971*b*) opt for a more passive or spurious relationship between delinquent associates and delinquency.

One way to gain insight into the importance of delinquent associates is to conduct a regression run with that variable omitted. The results of such a test are shown in Figure 5.6. The remaining variables approximately retain their original rank ordering (Table 5.1) in total causal effects on self-reported delinquent behavior. Delinquent values rank first with .38 total effects, followed by the school variables (school performance equals −.22; school attachment equals −.12), parental love (−.60), parental attachment (−.03), and occupational expectations (−.01). Perceived risks, susceptibility to peer influence, and social class (UC/EC) again have no effects.

The two important changes that occur when the regressions are run without delinquent associates are (*a*) a substantial decrease in R^2 and (*b*) a significant increase in the apparent effects of school performance. The latter finding indicates the importance of school performance in determining adolescent friendship choices. To some extent, then, the role of delinquent peers is passive. Having delinquent friends (like committing delinquent acts) is in part the consequence of school success and attachment to school. Those school variables are the only variables affecting delinquent associates in the original model (Figure 5.2), and school performance seems to take over some of the influence on delinquent behavior when delinquent associates are omitted (Figure 5.6).

Equally significant, however, is the loss in explained variation (R^2 drops from .27 to .20) when delinquent associates are dropped from the model.[14] If delinquent associates were merely another effect (along with illegal behavior) of school and parent ties, those attachment variables should be able to pick up the slack in explained variation when associates are omitted from the analysis. To the contrary, the decrease in R^2 from .27 to .20 represents a loss of 26 percent of the original explained variation because of the omission of delinquent associates. Clearly, delinquent (and nondelinquent) friends play an active role in producing (or preventing) law violation, above and beyond the verified tendency of birds of a feather to flock together.

Parallel analyses, comparing the reduction in R^2 for regression runs that omit each of the other independent variables one at a time, confirm the general ordering of the importance of variables found in Table 5.1. The omission of delinquent values reduces R^2 from .27 to .23, whereas each of the other omissions results in a loss of 1 percent of the explained variation or less. Additionally, eliminating the influence of both school variables or both parental variables fails to reduce the pre-

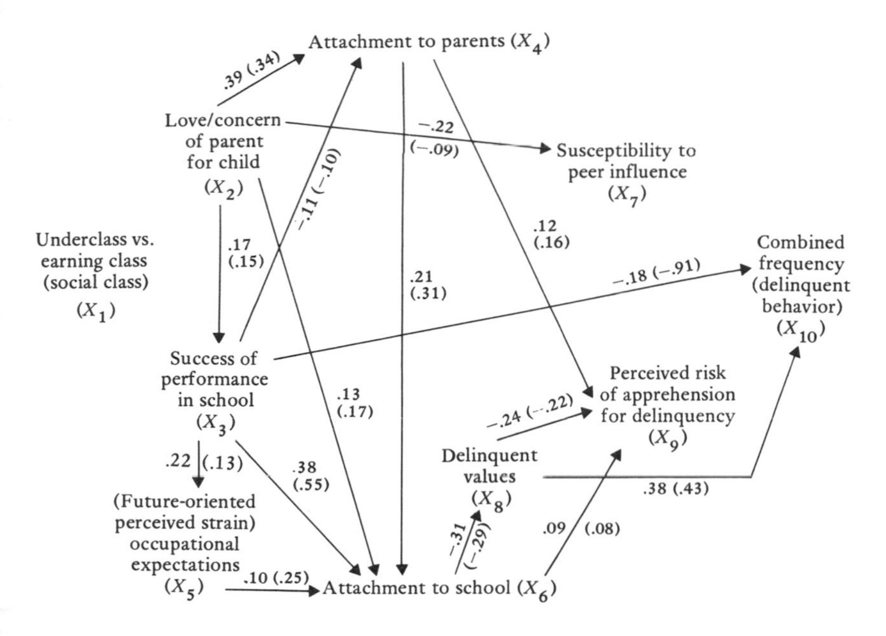

Figure 5.6. Results for the total sample ($N = 549$), including all paths with coefficients beyond $p < .01$, employing the following measures: underclass vs. earning class (X_1), occupational expectations (X_5), combined frequency (X_{11}). Delinquent associates are omitted from the model. ($R^2 = .20$)

diction power of the model. But the loss of both delinquent values and delinquent associates cuts the original R^2 from .27 to .11.

Delinquent values, then, as well as delinquent associates, appear to have a partly passive or spurious relevance to delinquent behavior, as well as an active role in its causation. However, school performance does not take over some of the effects on delinquent behavior when delinquent values are omitted (as is the case when delinquent associates are omitted). Rather, the original explanatory power of delinquent values either is lost (R^2 drops from .27 to .23) or is taken over by delinquent associates (whose standardized effects on law violation increase from .36 to .48). This finding argues for a closer relationship between school and associates than between school and values, which is consistent with the ordering in the model.

In summarizing the relative importance of the variables among the total sample of adolescents, the data indicate that differential association with delinquent peers and the adolescent's personal values toward delinquent behavior have the greatest total effects on delinquent behavior. But those two variables are themselves closely interrelated, and sorting out the place of each is a task yet to be accomplished. The so-called social ties to parents and school have lesser effects on delinquent behavior. In fact, perceived parental love and reported degree of attachment to a parent have almost no influence (directly or indirectly) on the extent of self-reported involvement in theft, vandalism, and assault.

Of the bonds that are commonly supposed to act as social constraints or to provide a stake in conformity, it is ties to school rather than to parents that are relevant among these adolescents. In fact, a social-bonding perspective suffers only to some extent from the finding of overall greater effects of delinquent associates and values: It seems that some portion of the effects of associates and values would be caused by school experiences if associates and values were omitted from the analysis.

And finally, several variables have virtually no influence on delinquent behavior in the model as specified. These include occupational expectations (from strain theory), social class, perceived risk of apprehension (from deterrence doctrine), and susceptibility to peer influence (without consideration for the delinquent involvement of those peers).

The problem of causal ordering

All of these conclusions regarding the relative importance of variables are valid only in the context of the specified model, including its assumptions of causal ordering. Path analysis (indeed, cross-sectional analysis in general) is severely limited as a means of demonstrating causal direction. Nonrecursive models are possible, provided that one has exogenous and/or lagged endogenous variables. And, of course, longitudinal data would be helpful in studying this issue. Both of those lines of inquiry should be pursued. But the present study is confined to cross-sectional data and a recursive model, and it therefore faces difficulties in asserting causal ordering. With the present data, this is most discomforting for the ordering between delinquent associates and delinquent values. This is a matter of concern partly because of the relatively strong effects of these variables on the dependent variable, combined with the high correlation ($r = .50$) between them, and partly because other authors have reversed the ordering in recent works (Liska, 1973; Hepburn, 1976).

Chapter 3 has presented the theoretical reasons for presuming that the impact of friendship formation (and therefore the degree of delinquent involvement of friends) on the adolescent's personal views of the acceptability of delinquent acts is greater than the influence of views on friendships. Here the focus is on what the data indicate. It has already been noted that delinquent associates are more closely related to prior school factors than are delinquent values. In fact, the R^2 of delinquent associates regressed on prior variables X_1 through X_6 is .18, compared to .10 for delinquent values regressed on those same variables. But again, this is extremely indirect support for the placing of delinquent associates closer to these prior variables in the causal scheme.[15]

Partial correlations among delinquent values, associates, and behavior all show reductions from simple correlations, but none reduces even halfway to zero. In short, there are no simple causal chains or totally spurious correlations among these three variables. In fact, it is simply impossible to determine empirically which comes first.

It is possible, however, to look at the consequences upon the apparent relative importance of values and associates of assuming the ordering in the model – rather than the opposite ordering. In other words, the apparent greater effects of delinquent associates could be the result of the assumption of their priority. In path analysis, any correlation between two variables (like values and associates) is viewed as the effect of whichever is presumed causally prior. Delinquent associates are therefore credited with having indirect effects on delinquent behavior – acting through delinquent values – because of the presumed sequence.

Figure 5.7 represents the results of presuming that delinquent values precede delinquent associates. Of course, the direct effects of the two variables on delinquent behavior are identical to those in the original run (Figure 5.2). The indirect effects are slightly less and are in this case attributed to delinquent values. The result is that the total causal effects of delinquent values (.38) and delinquent associates (.36) are virtually equal. Regardless of presumed causal ordering, then, delinquent associates are at least as influential as delinquent values in generating delinquent behavior. And finally, it is noteworthy that the direct effect from school performance to delinquent associates remains in Figure 5.7, this time controlling for the effects of delinquent values.

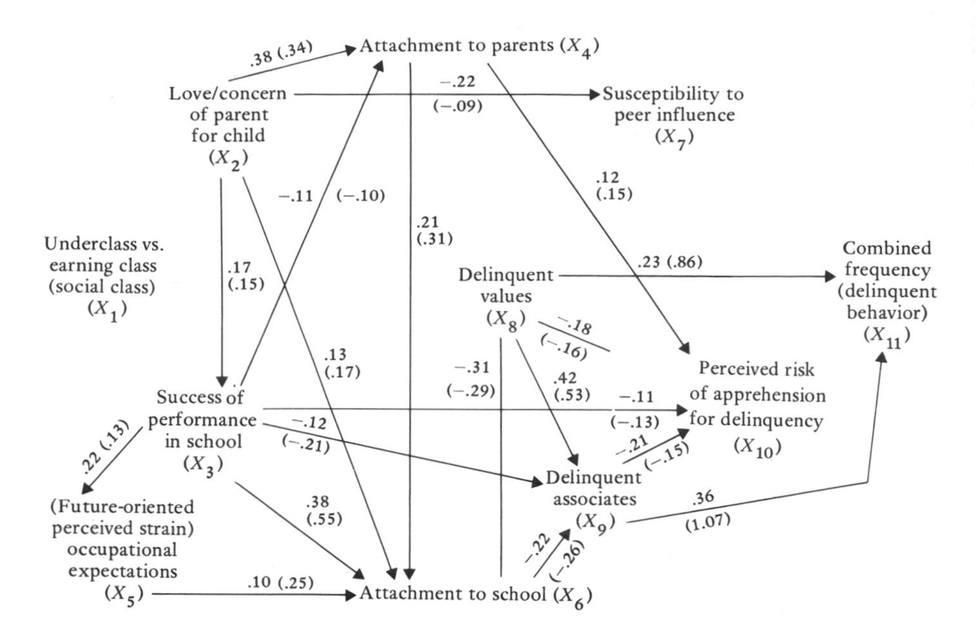

Figure 5.7. Results for the total sample ($N = 549$), including all paths with coefficients significant beyond $p < .01$, employing the following measures: underclass vs. earning class (X_1), occupational expectations (X_5), combined frequency (X_{11}). The causal ordering between delinquent associates and delinquent values is reversed. ($R^2 = .27$)

Given that the posited general conclusions about the relative importance of the variables seem justifiable even though it has not been possible to demonstrate causal direction empirically, it is now appropriate to turn to an examination of the extendability of these conclusions across subsamples. That is, are these generalizations comparably valid for males and females and for different types of delinquent activities? Or do the general findings mask some important interactions? The purpose of Chapter 6 is to look for the presence of those and other likely interactions.

6. Findings across subsamples

Causes for males and for females

Perhaps the most important and interesting test of the external validity of the findings entails a comparison of the results for males and for females. That is, do the inferred causal laws that were presented and considered in Chapter 5 operate in the same manner in the lives of adolescent boys and girls?

Carefully constructed theories of female delinquency as a special type of misbehavior do not seem to exist, largely because official statistics have shown relatively little female criminality (cf. Gibbons, 1976: 169–70). Self-report studies confirm that a moderately disproportional number of delinquent offenses are committed by males, but they also show quite extensive and generalized female involvement in illegalities, with similar patterns of offenses for both sexes (cf. Jensen and Eve, 1976; Hindelang, 1971*a;* Weis, 1973:370 ff.; Wise, 1967). The present data similarly show that the overall ratio of male-to-female frequency rates of delinquent behavior just exceeds 1.5:1. And the rank order of offenses most often admitted is the same for both sexes. But the point here is not to describe sex differences in behavior. The sample, in fact, lacks the representativeness required to do so accurately. The point is simply to make a case for a very general similarity in male and female offense patterns, to justify the presumption of a general similarity in causal mechanisms.

Some theorists, however, imply that certain factors are more relevant to female than to male delinquency. Specifically, "in one way or another, responsibility for most female delinquency is attributed to parental factors" (Gibbons, 1976:181; cf. Elliott and Voss, 1974). However, past evidence is contradictory.. Nye (1958:155) concludes that the role of parents as controls against deviance is indeed more salient for girls than for boys. Yet Schoenberg (1975:78, 82, 106) finds that affective ties to parents have less effect on delinquent associations and delinquent behavior in the female subsamples. Perhaps the more carefully delineated model used here will facilitate an understanding of this apparent contradiction.

The total sample has been divided into single race–sex subsamples for this analysis in order to avoid confounding possible sex and race differences. This breakdown results in too few cases in the black subsamples to obtain satisfactory path coefficient estimates. Hence, the examination of sex interactions will be based on whites and Asian Americans only. Figures 6.1 and 6.2 summarize the results for white males and females, respectively. The level of statistical significance required for inclusion in these diagrams is $p < .05$, less restrictive because of decreased sample size. The proper comparisons across subsamples now involve the *un*standardized regression coefficients (in parentheses), because of possible differences in variances. This, of course, entails the loss of the interpretability of coefficients in terms of explained variation.

There are numerous minor differences in the respective magnitudes (and in some cases in the significance) of the male and female coefficients, many undoubtedly attributable to sampling and measurement error. But most of the general patterns remain similar. Based on just the significant effects shown in Figures 6.1 and 6.2, for example, the total (direct plus indirect) *un*standardized effect of parental love on delinquent behavior is –.69 for males and –.43 for females. For males, then, those with one more point on the parental-love index scored (on the average) seven-tenths of one point (.69) less on the combined frequency of delinquency measure. The total unstandardized significant effects ($p < .05$) of all the variables on the delinquent behavior for white males and females are shown in Table 6.1. It is not appropriate to evaluate the relative importance of variables on the basis of Table 6.1. Differences in measurement scales make it impossible to compare a .75 effect of susceptibility to peer influence with a .53 effect of delinquent values, even within the same (white male) sample. Delinquent values are still much more important than susceptibility to peer influence, according to the standardized path coefficients shown in Table 6.2.

From Table 6.1 it seems that boys' delinquent involvement is more influenced than girls' by school performance, perceived parental love, attachment to parents, susceptibility to peer influence, delinquent associates, and perceived risk of apprehension.[1] On the other hand, attachment to school and delinquent values show greater relevance to female illegal behavior.

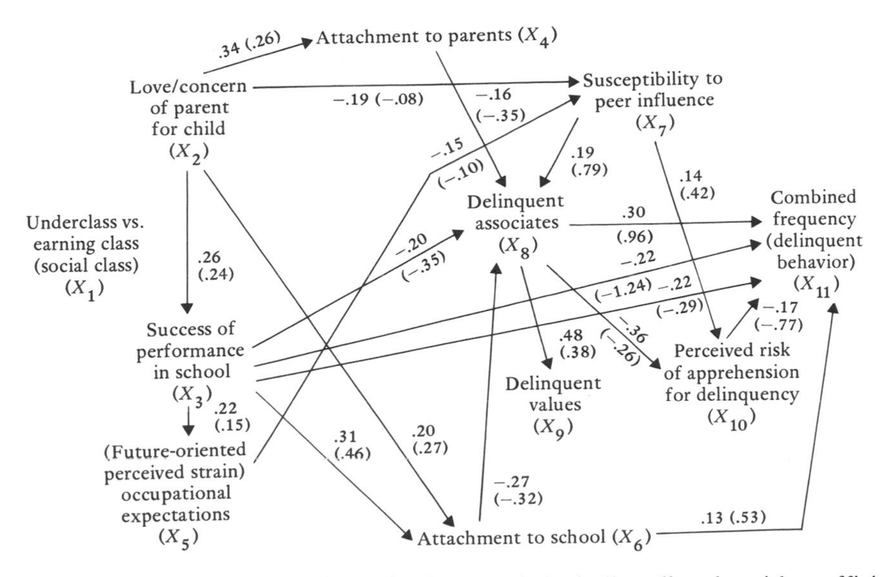

Figure 6.1. Results for white males ($N = 207$), including all paths with coefficients significant beyond $p < .05$, employing the following measures: underclass vs. earning class (X_1), occupational expectations (X_5), combined frequency (X_{11}). ($R^2 = .30$)

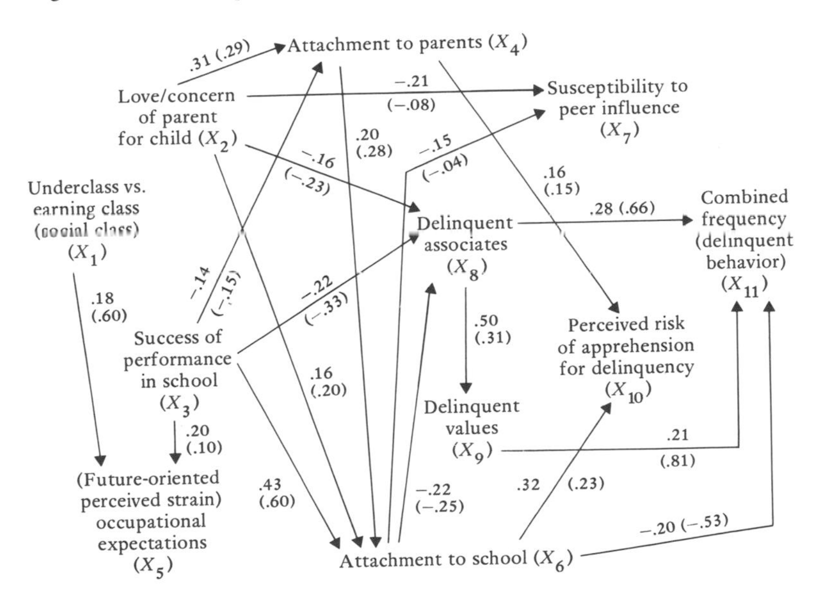

Figure 6.2. Results for white females ($N = 178$), including all paths with coefficients significant beyond $p < .05$, employing the following measures: underclass vs. earning class (X_1), occupational expectations (X_5), combined frequency (X_{11}). ($R^2 = .28$)

Table 6.1. *Total* unstandardized *effects of the causal variables on combined frequency of delinquent behavior for white males* (N = 207) *versus white females* (N = 178), *including all effects significant beyond* $p < .05$

Independent variable	Total effects for white males	Total effects for white females
Social class (UC/EC)	.00	.00
Parental love for child	-.69	-.43
School performance	-1.63	-.72
Attachment to parents	-.48	-.21
Occupational expectations	-.11	.00
Attachment to school	-.44	-.76
Susceptibility to peer influence	.75	.00
Delinquent associates	1.36	.91
Delinquent values	.53	.81
Perceived risk of apprehension	-.77	.00

Data from the smaller Asian samples are summarized in Tables 6.3 and 6.4 as a second check on the plausibility of tentative conclusions about sex differences based on the white samples. It would be unwise to use the Asian data for any more ambitious purpose. Because the sample sizes of Asian males ($N = 46$) and females ($N = 47$) are so small, all effects significant beyond $p < .20$ are included in Tables 6.3 and 6.4. There is therefore too great a risk of sampling error for these data to be utilized in drawing separate conclusions.

In combination with the white students' findings (Table 6.1), however, the Asian students' data (Table 6.3) support the proposition that the most consistent and/or strongest sex differences (in comparative magnitudes) in the absolute effects of the independent variables are as follows: Males show greater response to parental love, school performance, attachment to parents, and delinquent associates. Females show only a consistently greater absolute effect from delinquent values to delinquent behavior. Yet female values are not more influenced by prior variables (see Figures 6.1 and 6.2).

It is plausible that female adolescents feel a greater need to achieve cognitive balance with respect to delinquent values and activities than do males. That is, it may psychologically trouble girls, to a greater ex-

Table 6.2. *Rank orderings of the causal variables according to their total standardized effects on combined frequency of delinquent behavior, for white males* (N = 207) *and for white females* (N = 178), *including all effects significant beyond* $p < .05$

White males (R^2 = .30)	White females (R^2 = .28)
1. Delinquent associates (.42)	1. Delinquent associates (.38)
2. School performance (−.28)	2. School attachment (−.28)
3. Perceived risk (−.17)	3. Delinquent values (.21)
4. Delinquent values (.13)	4. School performance (−.20)
5. Parental love (−.08)	5. Parental love (−.12)
6. School attachment (−.11)	6. Parent attachment (−.06)
7. Parent attachment (−.07)	7. Perceived risk (.00)
8. Peer influence (.06)	8. Peer influence (.00)
9. Occup. expectations (−.01)	9. Occup. expectations (.00)
10. Social class (UC/EC) (.00)	10. Social class (UC/EC) (.00)

tent than boys, to do things they deem unacceptable. Indeed, perhaps that is one key to the sex difference in overall rates of illegalities. Even given equal values, females may find it more discomforting to violate those values in action. There is always the possibility, however, that females are instead more troubled by describing an act as unacceptable once they have done it (cf. Erickson and Smith, 1974). Thus the causal direction of this sex difference is somewhat equivocal, but the important difference remains as a candidate for future research.

With respect to the differential relevance of the school experience to male and female law violation, there seems to be a consistent sex difference in the magnitude of effects of school performance among both whites and Asians. That is, failure in school has a much greater delinquency-producing effect for boys than for girls. It is highly reasonable

Table 6.3. *Total unstandardized effects of the causal variables on combined frequency of delinquent behavior for Asian males* (N = 46) *versus Asian females* (N = 47), *including all effects significant beyond* $p < .20$

Independent variable	Total effects for Asian males	Total effects for Asian females
Social class (UC/EC)	-8.13	-5.01
Parental love for child	-.99	-.21
School performance	-3.89	-.30
Attachment to parents	-1.04	-.29
Occupational expectations	-3.93	-1.08
Attachment to school	-1.40	-.46
Susceptibility to peer influence	.00	-.56
Delinquent associates	2.42	.82
Delinquent values	-.26[a]	1.00
Perceived risk of apprehension	1.09[a]	.00

[a]This effect is in the opposite direction from that predicted by the theory.

that boys continue to feel greater pressure to succeeed in school in American society, to the extent that their degree of success in this respect has a direct significant bearing on the likelihood of delinquent involvement (see Figure 6.1). School success is evidently not as large a portion of a girl's stake in conformity and therefore not as relevant to her delinquent involvement.

With respect to parent-related controls, the finding of their greater relevance among males agrees with Schoenberg's 1975) findings. A justifiable conclusion here is that there is no evidence for the commonsense notion that parental ties and affection are somehow more important in generating female delinquent behavior.

Finally, the delinquent behavior of boys is more consistent with the delinquent behavior of their best friends than is the case with girls. Perhaps male law violations are more group and peer oriented. It seems that males have a greater need to be daring and to prove themselves to their friends in their search for masculine identity than do females in their search for feminine identity. At best, however, this is a post hoc interpretation of only a moderate difference in coefficients. It is certainly an issue that deserves closer attention in future research.

Table 6.4. *Rank orderings of the causal variables according to their total standardized effects on combined frequency of delinquent behavior, for Asian males* (N = 46) *and for Asian females* (N = 47), *including all effects significant beyond* $p < .20$.

Asian males (R^2 = .57)	Asian females (R^2 = .38)
1. School performance (-.52)	1. Delinquent associates (.39)
2. Delinquent associates (.50)	2. Delinquent values (.37)
3. School attachment (-.29)	3. School attachment (-.21)
4. Occup. expectations (-.24)	4. Social class (-.20)
5. Perceived risk (.18)[a]	5. Occup. expectations (-.16)
6. Social class (-.17)	6. Parent attachment (-.10)
7. Parental love (-.15)	7. School performance (-.09)
8. Parent attachment (-.14)	8. Parental love (-.08)
9. Delinquent values (-.07)[a]	9. Peer influence (-.08)
10. Peer influence (.00)	10. Perceived risk (.00)

[a]This effect is in the opposite direction from that predicted by the theory.

Shifting to the *standardized* coefficients allows for the examination of sex differences in the within-subsample relative effects of the variables among whites (Table 6.2) and Asians (Table 6.4). Once again, the data for whites are of greatest significance because of the larger sample. Table 6.2 shows that the conclusions drawn in Chapter 5 that delinquent associates have the greatest total effects on illegal involvement holds for white males and females. Only in the small Asian male sample does this variable fail to rank first in standardized influence, and there it is an extremely close second to school performance.

But this exception is important, for it highlights the greater relative importance that school performance has for males – a condition masked in the general analysis. That variable ranks second in total effects among white males and fourth among white females. (It ranks seventh, with virtually no influence, among Asian females). Therefore, school success not only has a greater absolute influence on illegal behavior among boys but also assumes a higher *relative* position for males in the hierarchy of causal factors. Omitting school performance from the model causes a loss of 13 percent of the original explained variation among white males but fails to affect the white female R^2.

In a similar fashion, delinquent values are both absolutely and relatively more efficacious among females of both races. And omitting the variable from the white female regressions reduces the original explained variation by 14 percent, compared to a 7 percent decline among white males.

The only other major sex differences in relative importance among whites (Table 6.2) are not consistent with the corresponding Asian findings (Table 6.4).

With sex differences in causal processes, then, it is best to limit conclusions to the more substantiated differences relating to the absolute and relative causal efficacy of delinquent values and school performance. A revision of the original causal model (Figure 5.1) should stress the role of delinquent values (and therefore the indirect rather than the direct influence of delinquent associates) in predicting female deviation. For males, it appears necessary to add a direct path from school performance to the dependent variable. Yet the general picture seems to remain very similar for both sexes. Differential associations play an active role in addition to their joint effects with social bonds, and within the realm of social controls the school is much more relevant than parent–child connections.

Origins of specific offenses

The small number of blacks and Asians in the sample makes it especially difficult to utilize their responses in searching for differences in the inferred causes of specific offenses.[2] Individual adolescents would become the sole bases for general conclusions. For example, only three Asian females have nonzero vandalism scores. Because of this difficulty, the analysis in this section is limited to white respondents. Even then there is the risk of having only slight variation in some dependent variables, so that the reader needs to recognize the sensitivity of these findings to sampling fluctuations.

Table 6.5. *Rank orderings of the total standardized effects of the causal variables on theft, vandalism, and assault for white males* (N = 209), *including all effects significant beyond* $p < .05$

Total effects on theft (R^2 = .24)	Total effects on vandalism (R^2 = .02)	Total effects on assault (R^2 = .09)
1. Delinquent assoc. (.40)	1. Social class (UC/EC) (–.15)	1. Delinquent values (.24)
2. School performance (–.25)	2.–10. All other variables have *no* effects.	2. Delinquent assoc. (.16)
3. Percieved risk (–.15)		3. Perceived risk (–.14)
4. Parental love (–.12)		4. School attachment (–.04)
5. School attachment (–.11)		5. Peer influence (.03)
6. Parent attachment (–.08)		6. Parental love (–.02)
7. Peer influence (.06)		7. Parent attachment (–.02)
8. Delinquent values (.00)		8. School performance (–.01)
9. Occup. expectations (.00)		9. Occup. expectations (–.01)
10. Social Class (UC/EC) (.00)		10. Social class (UC/EC) (.00)

As discussed early in Chapter 3, the general formulation is meant to apply to theft, vandalism, and violence with comparable tenability. However, parent–child ties were erroneously expected to play a greater role in the overall picture. Perhaps parents are more relevant to the generation of certain types of nonconformity. Several authors seem to imply, in fact, that parents are especially crucial in the causation of adolescent aggression or assault (Jenkins, 1957; Bandura and Walters, 1959; Berger and Simon, 1974:152). In summarizing past research findings, Gibbons (1976:200) states, "In short, scientific candor compels us to conclude that the link between parental rejection and aggressive conduct is one of the more firmly established generalizations concerning delinquency." Do the present data confirm the hypotheses that parents in general, and parental love in particular, are especially relevant to assaultive behavior?

Table 6.6. *Rank orderings of the total standardized effects of the causal variables on theft, vandalism, and assault for white females* (N = 179), *including all effects significant beyond* $p < .05$

Total effects on theft (R^2 = .27)	Total effects on vandalism (R^2 = .18)	Total effect on assault (R^2 = .13)
1. Delinquent assoc. (.36)	1. Social class (UC/EC) (−.26)	1. Delinquent assoc. (.36)
2. School attachment (−.29)	2. Occup. expectations (−.23)	2. School performance (−.11)
3. School performance (−.22)	3. Delinquent assoc. (.21)	3. School attachment (−.09)
4. Delinquent values (.21)	4. School performance (−.11)	4. Parental love (−.07)
5. Parental love (−.12)	5. School attachment (−.05)	5. Parent attachment (−.02)
6. Parent attachment (−.06)	6. Parental love (−.04)	6. Delinquent values (.00)
7. Perceived risk (.00)	7. Parent attachment (−.01)	7. Perceived risk (.00)
8. Peer influence (.00)	8. Delinquent values (.00)	8. Peer influence (.00)
9. Occup. expectations (.00)	9. Perceived risk (.00)	9. Occup. expectations (.00)
10. Social class (UC/EC) (.00)	10. Peer influence (.00)	10. Social class (UC/EC) (.00)

Table 6.5 summarizes the total standardized effects of the ten causal variables on the three separate types of illegalities for white males, and Table 6.6 does the same for white females. They include those effects significant beyond $p < .05$.

With respect to the role of parents in the causation of assaultive behavior, the data for both boys and girls fail to support the proposition that there is special relevance. The total effect of parental love in both samples is very small and ranks low in assault causation just as it does among the factors generating theft or vandalism. It seems that among the white males, however, the vandalism findings may have been washed out by sampling error because of minimal variation in the dependent variable. On the other hand, vandalism may simply be more spontaneous and less predictable behavior. Both interpretations are plausible.

In general, there is very little evidence of unique causal processes for specific types of offenses when both male and female data are considered. Among the boys those variables that seem to have special relevance to a particular type of offense (compared to effects on both other offense types) are: for theft - school performance; for vandalism - social class; and for assault - delinquent values. Among the girls, the uniquely high effects are: for theft - delinquent values; for vandalism - social class and occupational expectations; and for assault - none.

Of all these unique magnitudes of effects on particular types of offenses, only one is consistent across sex lines: Social class seems especially relevant (inversely) to vandalism, although the opposite conclusion - that the middle class is especially prone to property destruction rather than to theft or other serious illegalities - is usually drawn. But this finding of greater underclass vandalism is very tentative, because of so little variation in the variables. It is only ten underclass youths admitting medium vandalism and seven admitting large vandalism who give the small underclass sample a high vandalism rating.

In short, thc data fail to justify any conclusions about special mechanisms in the causation of different types of juvenile crime. This statement is not intended to downplay the findings of slight differences, however. They surely are leads for much needed exploration into the possibility of distinct antecedents for distinct kinds of delinquent acts (cf. Empey and Lubeck, 1971*a*:128). But at this point there is no compelling reason to deny the applicability of the general formulation across these types of offenses.

The effects of being labeled

In the theoretical discussion (Chapter 3), the possibility of feedback effects from official labeling as delinquent on what are supposed to be prior variables was briefly discussed. Perhaps the knowledge of being considered delinquent by others in fact *produces* lower occupational or educational expectations, a more delinquent value orientation, or other situations that lead to even greater delinquent activity (cf. Gold and Williams, 1969; Foster et al., 1972; Ageton and Elliott, 1974). If labeling is both an effect and then a cause of further delinquent behavior, then perhaps some of the inferred effects of other variables in previous interpretations are instead the sum of primary effects and the results of labeling feedback. For example, if the apparent effects of values on de-

Table 6.7. *Total* un*standardized effects of the causal variables on combined frequency of delinquent behavior for high labeled* (N = 97) *versus unlabeled* (N = 351) *among the total sample, including all effects significant beyond* $p < .05$ *for high labeled and* $p < .01$ *for unlabeled*

Independent variable	Total effects for high labeled (R^2 = .21)	Total effects for unlabeled (R^2 = .27)
Social class (UC/EC)	.00	.00
Parental love for child	.00	-.12
School performance	-1.80	-.40
Attachment to parents	.00	-.13
Occupational expectations	.00	.00
Attachment to school	.00	-.28
Susceptibility to peer influence	.00	.60
Delinquent associates	1.83	1.01
Delinquent values	.00	.86
Perceived risk of Apprehension	.00	.00

linquent behavior were very strong for labeled respondents and nonexistent for others, the presumed direction of influence from values to behavior would be in jeopardy. It would be more likely that the relationship was caused by the development of delinquent orientations (perhaps from resentment) by those who had been previously labeled, assuming a correlation between labeling and delinquent behavior.[3]

The present concern is not to test labeling theory. Rather, it is to determine if the general findings of Chapter 5 are equally applicable to those who have and who have not been in official trouble for delinquent activities. Consequently, separate regression runs were conducted for all "unlabeled" (labeled variable equals zero; see the Appendix) and "highly labeled" (labeled variable equals two or more) adolescents. The *un*standardized total effects are shown in Table 6.7. Statistical significance required for inclusion differs because there are more unlabeled (N = 351) than highly labeled (N = 97) respondents. Unstandardized coefficients allow for comparisons of the importance of the same measure across the two samples, but not of the relative importance of variables within either sample.

There appear to be substantial differences between the two subsamples in the absolute effects of the following variables: school performance, school attachment, susceptibility to peer influence, and delinquent values. However, the differences in all but school performance are entirely the result of a coefficient of a certain magnitude barely exceeding the significance criterion for one sample and barely missing the criterion for the other. In short, the only meaningful difference is that school failure is much more closely related to delinquent behavior among the highly labeled students.

Given only a moderate correlation between frequency of delinquent behavior and degree of labeling ($r = .30$), not all of this apparently special effect of school performance among the labeled can be attributed to feedback from delinquent behavior. In a related study, for example, Fisher (1972) finds no effects of delinquent labeling on school performance. Perhaps slightly greater reciprocal causation between school performance and law violation among the labeled does in fact cause an overestimation of the role of school performance in generating early misbehavior. On the other hand, questionnaire items about school success were intentionally worded in the past tense. Moreover, it is plausible that the actual effects of school performance vary by absolute level of school performance (a nonlinearity), for the labeled also show less school success ($r = -.21$ between the following variables, labeled and success of performance in school, as scored in the Appendix). School performance may become especially relevant to delinquent behavior for those closer to flunking out.

These complications and the possibilities of interactions, feedbacks, and nonlinearities certainly deserve more detailed specialized research. But the general formulation seems to remain tenable in spite of these circumstances. The greater importance of associations and values than attachments in delinquency causation is unaffected by the presence or absence of labeling. And the possibility of reciprocal or nonlinear relationships between school performance and delinquent behavior does not alter the conclusion that the data show the school to be more salient to law violations than are parent–child relationships.

The special case of the slums

Perhaps it is appropriate to conclude the analysis where it all began, with a final check for the presence of some implications from social class-related theories. As discussed in the introductory chapter, strain and subculture theories imply that different processes operate in different segments of the class structure in the etiology of delinquent behavior. The present findings of no class effects on any other variable under consideration argue against such differences. However, there remains the logical possibility that the effect of class position is to condition the nature of interrelationships among the more relevant variables. That is, distinct causal laws could lead to similar behavior rates in the separate (underclass versus earning-class) social strata.

One specific implication of subcultural theories (especially Miller's, 1958) is that the roles of parents and values may differ by social class. If underclass parents socialize their offspring with delinquent values, then parental attachment in that social sector should *increase* delinquent values, associates, and behavior.

As one might expect, there is no evidence of such class-specific subcultural effects. In the first place, class (UC/EC) and parental delinquent values (a one-item measure; see the Appendix) are unrelated ($r = -.05$, $p < .12$). Furthermore, separate regression runs with only underclass respondents, and with only those respondents whose parents are reported to hold delinquent values, fail to reveal any unusual effects.[4] Perceived parental love still leads to attachment to parents, which continues to have moderate positive effects on school attachment and consequent indirect negative effects on delinquent associates, values, and behavior.

In short, there are no apparent differences in the causal processes within the underclass and/or the delinquent-parental-values subsamples. Of course, the proportion of underclass adolescents is very small. On the basis of all the data, however, there is no reason to question the generalizability of the previous conclusions to samples involving greater numbers of underclass adolescents or of adolescents whose parents fail to espouse conventional values.

The interactions discussed in this chapter represent only a few of the numerous nonadditive and/or nonlinear relationships that could exist among this set of variables. Path analysis simply does not detect these more complex kinds of relationships, unless numerous product terms are inserted in a blind search for evidence of interactions. The present study employed path analysis only to check for the presence of specifically foreseen difficulties. With respect to those that were foreseen and examined in this chapter, the general sense of the overall conclusions of

Chapter 5 does not seem to depend upon the sex, social class, labeling status, or parental-values stance of, or the kinds of offenses committed by, the adolescent.

The several minor ways in which these considerations condition the magnitudes of important relationships are best seen as insights for further research, rather than as serious threats to the usefulness of the integrated causal model.

A summary of all the major findings follows in Chapter 7. It attempts to tie the empirical results together and to link them with the theoretical discussions found in the first three chapters.

7. Origins of juvenile delinquency: a final statement

An initial examination of the major competing theoretical orientations to delinquent behavior leads to the conclusion that each formulation contains insights into the etiology of delinquent behavior. This monograph represents an attempt to incorporate the most promising insights from the various perspectives into a single causal model and to test the model's tenability with original data.

On the basis of past research, a list of variables with seemingly general relevance to self-reported delinquent behavior was developed in Chapter 2. These included social class as measured by an underclass/earning-class dichotomy (UC/EC), parent–child relationships, school experiences, future-oriented strain or frustration, delinquent associates, delinquent values, and deterrence through fear of threatened punishment.

These general factors were refined and woven into an explicit causal scheme in Chapter 3, with Figure 3.10 representing the resulting theoretical model. Double arrows signify expectations of greater causal efficacy, and the dashed arrow represents a proposed conditioning or interaction effect. The model can be characterized as an attachment brand of social control theory with an appreciation for differential association processes, or vice versa. Moreover, it incorporates social class and deterrence as well. It is above all an integrated formulation.

The propositions entailed in the causal model were tested, using the measures and techniques described in Chapter 4. Multiple indexes were developed for many of the concepts, and special care was taken to avoid conceptual confusion through multicollinearity. In the process, the model was revised into a more testable version (Figure 5.1) through the incorporation of anticipated peer approval for delinquency into the delinquent associates construct.

The model includes several variable clusters that derive from major theoretical traditions in the field of juvenile delinquency. Specifically, strain, subculture, and control (bonding) theories contain predictions or

Table 7.1. *Summary of the relative importance of the major variable clusters, as implied by theoretical traditions and as found in this research*

	Variables with central or primary influence	Variables with moderate or indirect effects	Variables of little or no importance
Strain perspective	Future-oriented strain Social class	School experiences	Delinquent associates Delinquent values Parent–child relationships
Subculture perspective	Social class Delinquent associates Delinquent values	School experiences	Future-oriented strain Parent–child relationships
Control (bonding) perspective	Parent–child relationships School experiences	Delinquent values	Social class Future-oriented strain Delinquent associates
Research findings	Delinquent associates Delinquent values School experiences	Parent–child relationships	Social class Future-oriented strain

implications about the roles of the following in delinquency causation: social class, parent–child relationships, school experiences, future-oriented strain, delinquent associates, and delinquent values.[1] Table 7.1 summarizes the implied importance of these variable clusters within each of the three theoretical traditions. An explanation of why any particular variable is entered as it is can be found in Chapters 1 and 2. The final row in Table 7.1 summarizes the relative empirical importance of the variable clusters as found in this research. Together these variables

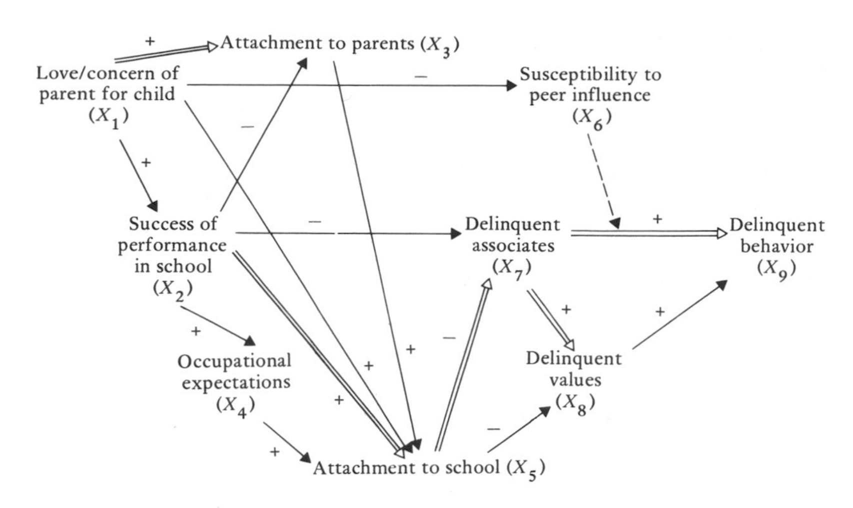

Figure 7.1. The empirically supported model

explain 27 percent of the variation in self-reported theft, vandalism, and assault. This figure compares favorably with that obtained in other studies but also indicates the great need for theoretical and methodological advances in this area of inquiry.

In comparing the theories with the findings, the most obvious conclusion is that strain notions fail quite dramatically. Social class and perceptions of future failure are simply not related to self-reported illegalities in the present sample. The best theory would appear to be a combination of a class-free subculture (i.e., social learning) perspective with a social bonding orientation.

In essence, that combination is what is represented in Figure 7.1, a diagram of the empirically supported portions of the original model. At this point the reader should recall that the purpose throughout this monograph has been to integrate the theories, rather than to have them compete with one another. Thus the interrelationships depicted in Figure 7.1 are more central to a summary of findings than are the listings in Table 7.1.

On the basis of the general findings described in Chapter 5, social class and perceived risk of apprehension are omitted from the revised model. And future-oriented perceived strain is reconceptualized as commitment to conventional work patterns, measured by occupational expectations. There is simply no evidence that frustrations deriving from anticipated career failures drive adolescents to delinquent behavior.

Given the assumptions regarding the ordering of the variables, delinquent associates have the greatest influence on law violation in the final model. Moreover, this effect is accentuated when increased desire for peer approval produces a rise in susceptibility to peer influence. Delinquent values also play a relatively powerful role. It seems that it is appropriate and useful to conceptualize a continuum of values in relation to the acceptability of certain illegal acts, rather than to expect adolescents to espouse *either* conventional *or* deviant values.

School ties are quite important, but parent attachments seem to play only a minor role in the overall causal scheme, in contrast to original expectations. By the time they reach adolescence, at least, these young people's situational decisions to abide by or break the law are almost unaffected by the nature of their ties with their parents.

However, longitudinal studies might reveal greater effects of *early* parent–child interaction on the later likelihood of delinquent associates and values. Even wording parental-love items in the past tense, as was done in this research, cannot really recapture a specific earlier time. Perhaps there is some crucial period in a child's life during which his or her experiences with mother and/or father are quite predictive of later misbehavior, but the generalized drifting away from parents during adolescence may mask these effects, using cross-sectional data. This is, of course, speculation. But the findings point with great force to the need for longitudinal research into the effects of parents on delinquent behavior.

Other findings of Chapter 5 similarly indicate fruitful fields for future inquiry. The role of parental love in determining susceptibility to peer influence, for example, deserves exploration as another way that parents may indeed be more relevant than the general findings seem to indicate.

The data further suggest that the causal efficacy of personal values (not shown in Figure 7.1) may be greater for more serious offenses, an implication deserving further testing with offense-specific data. And finally, the general findings should not constitute the end of testing for class (UC/EC) and deterrence propositions. The UC/EC conceptualization deserves a test in a sample with a larger number of underclass respondents. And perceived certainty of punishment may in fact deter, given specific crimes and/or given a threshold level of adequate certainty.

The exploration of possible complications and interactions in Chapter 6 provides further suggestions for potentially valuable research, as well as insights in itself. There are indications that within the general context of the same causal model, values are perhaps more salient for females and school performance more salient for males in determining the likelihood of illegal activities.

The need for further research is also indicated by the apparent special effect of school performance on the delinquent behavior of those who happen to have been in trouble with authorities. It is possible that school performance is especially relevant to law violation when school success is very low (a nonlinear relationship) and/or that some of the inferred effects of school performance are in reality the feedback effects of official labeling. Perhaps teachers are less likely to expect and therefore to find merit in the schoolwork of "troublemakers." And the adolescents who know they are so identified are probably less likely to put forth the effort required to succeed.

All of these qualifications and refinements, however, do not singly or jointly negate the tenability of the general conclusions. Moreover, the range of applicability of the formulation - its external validity - is supported by the findings of similar causal processes for various types of offenses, in separate social sectors (UC/EC), and for adolescents whose parents seem to hold delinquent values.

The incorporation of often unrelated or competing conceptions and propositions has led to a tenable general theory of involvement in delinquent behavior. In addition to the insights hereby gained about the relative importance and interrelationships of selected variables in the causation of delinquent behavior, it is hoped that the model represents a springboard for future research. That research should move toward further clarification of the processes considered here, toward the search for and incorporation of other variables into the overall scheme, and toward refinements in the specification of conditioning effects of other variables that alter the causal processes in given situations.

Appendix: The measuring devices

This Appendix contains the scoring techniques used to derive the various index scores from responses to individual questionnaire items. The specific indexes are grouped under the appropriate general concept. The general concepts requiring measurement (listed immediately below) are discussed in the Appendix in alphabetical order. The information in this Appendix is meant to supplement the descriptions of the measures in the text rather than to stand alone as a complete delineation of measurement methods. Index scores are *sums* of the scores for responses to the composite items unless otherwise stated.

Theoretical construct

I Attachment to parents
II Attachment to school
III Caring what parents think
IV Delinquent associates
V Delinquent behavior
VI Delinquent parental values
VII Delinquent values
VIII Future-oriented perceived strain
IX Labeled
X Love/concern of parent for child
XI Perceived risk of apprehension for delinquency
XII Social class
XIII Success of performance in school
XIV Susceptibility to peer influence

I.

Attachment to parents

Father attachment[1]

19. Who is now acting as "father" for you?
(23)
____ (1) Real father
____ (2) Stepfather
____ (3) Foster father
____ (4) Grandfather
____ (5) Other relative
____ (6) Other unrelated adult male
____ (7) No one[2]

20. Is your father (or adult male guardian) living at home with you?
(24)
2 (1) Yes
1 (2) Sometimes
0 (3) No
0 (4) I have no father

	(1) Strongly agree	(2) Agree	(3) Undecided	(4) Disagree	(5) Strongly Disagree
27. (29) I'm closer to my father than are most people my age.	2	1	0	0	0
28. (30) As an adult, I want to live near where my father will be living.	2	1	0	0	0

	(1) Always	(2) Usually	(3) Sometimes	(4) Seldom	(5) Never
37. (41) When I have problems I confide in my father.	2	1	0	0	0

39. When I have free time I spend it with my father.	2	1	0	0	0

II.

Attachment to school

	(1) Strongly agree	(2) Agree	(3) Unde- cided	(4) Dis- agree	(5) Strongly Dis- agree
4. Homework is a waste of time.	0	0	0	1	2
5. I try hard in school.	2	1	0	0	0
7. Education is so important it's worth it to put up with things about school that I don't like.	2	1	0	0	0

11. Do you like school in general?
 2 (1) Very much
 1 (2) Somewhat
 0 (3) Hardly
 0 (4) Not at all

12. Do you care what teachers think of you?
 2 (1) Very much
 1 (2) Somewhat
 0 (3) Hardly
 0 (4) Not at all

13. How important are grades to you personally?
 2 (1) Very important
 1 (2) Somewhat important

_0_ (3) Hardly important
_0_ (4) Not at all important

14. Do you finish your homework?
_0_ (1) Never
_0_ (2) Seldom
_0_ (3) Sometimes
_1_ (4) Usually
_2_ (5) Always

III.

Caring what parents think

22. Do you care what your father thinks of you?
_3_ (1) Very much
_2_ (2) Somewhat
_1_ (3) Hardly
_0_ (4) Not at all
_–_ (5) I have no father.

26. Do you care what your mother thinks of you?
_3_ (1) Very much
_2_ (2) Somewhat
_1_ (3) Hardly
_0_ (4) Not at all
_–_ (5) I have no mother.

The total score on caring what parents think is the greater (not the sum) of these two scores.

IV

Delinquent associates

72. Not counting traffic tickets, how many of your best friends have ever been picked up by the police?
_0_ (1) None
_1_ (2) One
_2_ (3) Two
_3_ (4) More than two (please estimate the actual number ___)

_–_ (5) Don't know

74. As far as you know, have your best friends been involved in any illegal activities in the past year?
 _0_ (1) Never
 _1_ (2) Seldom
 _2_ (3) Sometimes
 _3_ (4) Frequently
 _1_ (5) Don't know
 _0_ (6) Don't have any best friends

75. Among your best friends, is doing something that is daring but illegal ever rewarded with approval or congratulations?
 _3_ (1) Always
 _2_ (2) Usually
 _1_ (3) Sometimes
 _0_ (4) Seldom
 _0_ (5) Never

76. If you were shoplifting and your best friends saw you, would you be embarrassed?
 _0_ (1) Yes, and ashamed
 _0_ (2) Yes, somewhat
 _1_ (3) Maybe a little bit
 _2_ (4) Not at all

77. As far as you know, do your best friends *disapprove* of breaking the law?
 _0_ (1) Very much
 _0_ (2) Somewhat
 _1_ (3) Hardly
 _2_ (4) Not at all

V

Delinquent behavior

A. Theft

For each question, zero to ten are scored with the actual number; eleven or more times are scored twenty.

54. In the past year have you taken things of small value (worth less than $5) that did not belong to you?

56. In the past year have you taken things of some value (worth between $5 and $50) that did not belong to you?

58. In the past year have you taken things of large value (worth more than $50) that did not belong to you?

64. In the past year have you taken a car for a ride without the owner's permission?

B. Vandalism

For each question, zero to ten times are scored with the actual number; eleven or more times are scored twenty.

60. In the past year have you banged up or destroyed things of some value (worth between $5 and $50) that did not belong to you on purpose?

62. In the past year have you banged up or destroyed things of large value (worth more than $50) that did not belong to you on purpose?

C. Assault

For each question, zero to ten times are scored with the actual number; eleven or more times are scored twenty.

66. Not counting fights you may have had with your brother or sister, have you beaten up or hurt anyone on purpose in the past year?

67. In the past year have you attacked someone with a weapon other than your fists, willing to injure the person seriously if it came to that?

D. Combined frequency

The combined frequency-of-delinquent-behavior score is the simple sum of the theft, vandalism, and assault totals.

E. Combined seriousness

The combined seriousness-of-delinquent-behavior score is based on the theft, vandalism, and assault scores. Item fifty-four (small theft) is omitted. The frequency responses (one to ten, twenty) to items fifty-six (medium theft) and sixty (medium vandalism) are summed. Then the frequency responses to items fifty-eight (large theft), sixty-two (large vandalism), and sixty-six (simple assault) are each multiplied by a factor of two and the products are added to the sum. The frequency response to item sixty-seven (serious assault) is multiplied by three and the product is added to the sum. Finally, the frequency response to item sixty-four (car theft) is multiplied by two and the product is added to the seriousness sum, *unless* item sixty-five is answered by one of the asterisked responses, in which case no value is added for car theft.

65. If you answered yes, who was the owner of the *last* such car you took?

__*__ (1) A relative
__*__ (2) A friend
____ (3) A neighbor
____ (4) A casual acquaintance
____ (5) A stranger
__*__ (No response to item sixty-five)

VI

Delinquent parental values

97. How would your parents feel if they happened to see you shoplifting?

__1__ (1) Very upset
__2__ (2) Somewhat upset
__3__ (3) Hardly bothered
__4__ (4) Proud of me if I didn't get caught
__–__ (5) Don't know

VIII

Delinquent values

Please mark how often each of the following actions seems acceptable to you.

	(1) Never	(2) Seldom	(3) Sometimes	(4) Usually	(5) Always
106. Fistfighting	0	0	1	2	3
107. Taking something of small value from a rich person	0	0	1	2	3
108. Destroying school property	0	0	1	2	3
109. Sneaking into a movie or ball game without paying	0	0	1	2	3
110. Physically hurting someone	0	0	1	2	3

	(1) Strongly Agree	(2) Agree	(3) Undecided	(4) Disagree	(5) Strongly Disagree
111. It's okay to get around the law if you can get away with it.	2	1	0	0	0

VIII

Future-oriented perceived strain

A. Occupational expectations

84. Write the number which is in front of the type of job coming closest to describing the kind of work you *realistically expect* as your career or "life's work": ____ (number)

Manual work (blue collar)	*Examples*
(1) Domestic	housecleaning, maid, babysitter, daycare worker
(2) Laborer	construction worker, janitor, helper
(3) Semi-skilled	machine operator, truck driver, assembly line
(4) Craftsman	journeyman carpenter, electrician, plumber, jeweler
(5) Foreman	foreman of a work gang, factory inspector
White collar	
(6) Semiskilled	store clerk, mail carrier, salesman
(7) Skilled	secretary, bookkeeper, court clerk
(8) Entertainer	actor, athlete, model
(9) Professional	doctor, lawyer, architect, teacher, social worker
(10) Manager	executive, superintendent, editor, senator
(11) Merchant	owner of small store or small company
(12) Large business	owner of large store, company, or factory
Other	
(13) Farmer	owner of farm or ranch
(14) Housewife	taking care of own home – not for pay
(15) Unemployed	
(16) Deceased	
(17) Don't know	
(18) Don't care	

Five levels of occupational expectations were then created from categories one through twelve. The lowest level (unskilled) is scored one and includes categories one and two. The score is two (semi-skilled) for category three. The score is three (skilled manual) for categories four, five, and eleven. The score is four (white-collar) for categories six and seven. And the score is five (professional/executive) for categories eight, nine, ten, and twelve.

B. Educational expectations

17. Realistically, how much education do you think you will *actually get?*

  1   (1) Some high school or less
  2   (2) High school graduate
  3   (3) High school plus trade or business school
  4   (4) Some college, without graduating
  5   (5) Four-year college graduate
  6   (6) College plus graduate school

C. Worry about future career

88. Do you worry about getting a decent "life's work" in the future?

  3   (1) Very much
  2   (2) Some
  1   (3) Hardly any
  0   (4) Not at all

D. Perceived barriers to future success

18. Check *as many* of the following reasons that seem like they may prevent you from getting as much education as you really desire.

  1   (1) I don't have the needed abilities.
  1   (2) I don't have the needed money.
  1   (3) I just won't get the breaks.
  1   (4) This school doesn't give me the training I would need.
  1   (5) They don't want "my kind" in that type of school.
  *   (6) I just don't care that much.[3]

85. Check *as many* of the following reasons that seem like they may prevent you from getting the type of job you really want.

  1   (1) I don't have the needed abilities.
  1   (2) I don't have the needed money.
  1   (3) I just won't get the breaks.
  1   (4) This school doesn't give me the training I would need.
  1   (5) They don't want "my kind" in a job like that.
  *   (6) I just don't care that much.

It should be noted that the total barriers score is a sum of individual *response* scores, not of item scores. That is, the subject may respond to as many of the choices as apply for these particular items, making the maximum barriers score ten.

E. Occupational aspirations/expectations discrepancy

Expectations are measured on a scale of one to five as described in the section on occupational expectations. Aspirations are measured along the same one-to-five scale, utilizing the same job categories, by means of item eighty-three:

83. Write the number which is in front of the type of job coming closest to describing the kind of work you would do if you were allowed to *choose any job or occupation you desired:* ____ (number)

Any difference between the aspirations and expectations scores is counted as one point on this index. Added to this base are the points indicated for certain responses to items eighty-six through eighty-eight:

86. How serious are you about wanting the type of job you chose above as being *most desirable* to you?
    2 (1) It's what I've always wanted to be.
    1 (2) Few other types of work would satisfy me as much.
    0 (3) I haven't thought about it much, but it sounds like good work.
    * (4) It's really just a wild dream.

87. How much time have you spent seriously considering what you will do after high school?
    * (1) None at all
    * (2) Hardly any
    0 (3) Some
    1 (4) Very much

88. Do you worry about getting a decent "life's work" in the future?
    2 (1) Very much
    1 (2) Some
    0 (3) Hardly any
    * (4) Not at all

Next, points are added for perceptions of barriers to occupational success. Of the first five responses to item eighty-five, one point is added if one or two responses are marked and two are added if three to five responses are checked.

85. Check *as many* of the following reasons that seem like they may prevent you from getting the type of job you really want.
    1 (1) I don't have the needed abilities.
    1 (2) I don't have the needed money.
    1 (3) I just won't get the breaks.
    1 (4) This school doesn't give me the training I would need.
    1 (5) They don't want "my kind" in a job like that.
    * (6) I just don't care that much.

Finally, the total index score is set at zero if the respondent's *labeled* index score (see the *labeled* section of this Appendix) exceeds six *and* he or she marks response three or five on item eighty-five.

F. Educational aspirations/expectations discrepancy

The expectations score ranges from one to six as described above in the section on educational expectations. The level of aspirations is measured on the same one-to-six scale from the responses given to the following item:

16. If you could have *as much as you desired,* how much education would you choose to get?
    1 (1) Some high school or less
    2 (2) High school graduate
    3 (3) High school plus trade or business school
    4 (4) Some college, without graduating
    5 (5) Four-year college graduate
    6 (6) College plus graduate school

If expectations equal or exceed aspirations, the total discrepancy score is zero. If aspirations are greater, the expectation score is subtracted from the aspiration score. Points are added to this difference from item eighteen as follows: one point is added for a sum of one or two responses to choices one through five. Two are added for a sum of three to five responses to choices one through five. Marking choice six on item eighteen makes the *entire* discrepancy score equal zero.

18. Check as many of the following reasons that seem like they may prevent you from getting as much education as you really desire.
  1 (1) I don't have the needed abilities.
  1 (2) I don't have the needed money.
  1 (3) I just won't get the breaks.
  1 (4) This school doesn't give me the training I would need.
  1 (5) They don't want "my kind" in that type of school.
  * (6) I just don't care that much.

IX

Labeled

15. Have you ever been suspended from school?
  0 (1) Never
  1 (2) Once
  2 (3) Twice
  3 (4) Three times
  3 (5) More than three times

51. Not counting traffic tickets, have you ever been picked up by the police?
  0 (1) Never
  1 (2) Once
  2 (3) Twice
  3 (4) Three or more times (please estimate actual number ____)

52. Have you ever had to go to juvenile court for something you did?
  0 (1) Never
  1 (2) Once
  2 (3) Twice
  3 (4) Three or more times (please estimate actual number ____)

X

Love/concern of parent for child

Father love[4]

	(1) Always	(2) Usually	(3) Sometimes	(4) Seldom	(5) Never
31. (41) It has been hard for me to please my father.	0	0	0	1	2
33. (43) My father has ridiculed or made fun of my ideas.	0	0	0	1	2
34. (44) My father has trusted me.	2	1	0	0	0
36. (46) My father has seemed to wish I were a different type of person.	0	0	0	1	2

XI

Perceived risk of apprehension for delinquency

101. What do you think would be your *personal chances of getting caught* if you were shoplifting?
    - 5 (1) Very high (75%–100%)
    - 4 (2) Moderately high (50%–74%)
    - 3 (3) Somewhat low (25%–49%)
    - 2 (4) Quite low (10%–24%)
    - 1 (5) Very low (less than 10%)

102. What do you think would be your personal chances of getting caught if you were breaking school windows at 8:00 P.M.?

5 (1) Very high (75%–100%)
4 (2) Moderately high (50%–74%)
3 (3) Somewhat low (25%–49%)
2 (4) Quite low (10%–24%)
1 (5) Very low (less than 10%)

XII

Social Class

A. SES of father's occupation

89. Please write the name of your father's job in this space, along with a few words describing what he does in his job.

From responses to this open-ended item, I coded the father's occupation into one of the five levels described in the occupational-expectations section of this Appendix (found in the general section on future-oriented perceived strain).

B. Underclass zero versus earning class one

To be categorized as underclass (and scored zero on the dichotomous UC/EC variable) the respondent must meet several criteria: low income, *and* employment or welfare, *and* both parents low in education or both parents low in occupation. The specific responses that meet these criteria are marked with an X for the items below:

Low income

96. How would you honestly describe your parents' total income?
X (1) Poverty level
X (2) Somewhat below average
____ (3) Average
____ (4) Somewhat above average
____ (5) Wealthy

Unemployment

39. Please write the name of your father's job in this space, along with

a few words describing what he does in his job.
_X_ Unemployed (as coded by me)
(or)

90. How much time during the past three years has your father been out of work *because he could not find a job?*
  ____ (1) None at all
  _X_ (2) Less than six months
  _X_ (3) 6 months–1 year
  _X_ (4) 1 year–2 years
  _X_ (5) More than two years
  ____ (6) I have no father.
  ____ (7) Don't know

(or)

21. Is your father (or adult male guardian) now working?
  ____ (1) Yes, full-time
  _X_ (2) Yes, part-time
  _X_ (3) No, he's looking for a job.
  _X_ (4) No, he keeps house.
  _X_ (5) No, he's ill or disabled.
  _X_ (6) No, he's retired.
  _X_ (7) No, for some other reason
  ____ (8) I have no father.

Welfare

95. Has your family ever received any welfare benefits?
  ____ (1) Never
  _X_ (2) Only in the past year
  _X_ (3) Only more than a year ago
  _X_ (4) This past year *and* more than a year ago
  _X_ (5) I'm not sure.

Low parental education

93. How much education has your father had?
  _X_ (1) Some high school or less
  _X_ (2) High school graduate

_X_ (3) High school plus trade or business school
_X_ (4) Some college, without graduating
____ (5) Four-year college graduate
____ (6) College plus graduate school
____ (7) I have no father.
____ (8) Don't know

94. How much education has your mother had?
_X_ (1) Some high school or less
_X_ (2) High school graduate
_X_ (3) High school plus trade or business school
_X_ (4) Some college, without graduating
____ (5) Four-year college graduate
____ (6) College plus graduate school
____ (7) I have no mother.
____ (8) Don't know

Low parental occupation

This includes any responses to open-ended items eighty-nine and ninety-one that I coded as one, two, three, four, five, eleven, fourteen, fifteen, or sixteen according to the criteria detailed in the list that follows:

89. Please write the name of your father's job in this space, along with a few words describing what he does in his job.
91. Please write the name of your mother's job in this space, along with a few words describing what she does in her job.

Manual work (blue collar)	*Examples*
X(1) Domestic	housecleaning, maid, babysitter, day-care worker
X(2) Laborer	construction worker, janitor, helper
X(3) Semiskilled	machine operator, truck driver, assembly line
X(4) Craftsman	journeyman carpenter, electrician, plumber, jeweler
X(5) Foreman	foreman of a work gang, factory inspector
White collar	
(6) Semiskilled	store clerk, mail carrier, salesman
(7) Skilled	secretary, bookkeeper, court clerk

(8) Entertainer	actor, athlete, model
(9) Professional	doctor, lawyer, architect, teacher, social worker
(10) Manager	executive, superintendent, editor, senator
X(11) Merchant	owner of small store or small company
(12) Large business	owner of large store, company, or factory

Other

(13) Farmer	owner of farm or ranch
X(14) Housewife	taking care of own home – not for pay
X(15) Unemployed	
X(16) Deceased	
(17) Don't know	
(18) Don't care	

Finally, if the respondent reported having no one acting as father (item nineteen, response seven), the following mother items were substituted for an indication of parental unemployment, with the specific responses marked with an X.

25. Is your mother (or adult female guardian) now working?
____ (1) Yes, full-time
_X_ (2) Yes, part-time
_X_ (3) No, she's looking.
_X_ (4) No, she keeps house.
_X_ (5) No, she's ill or disabled.
_X_ (6) No, she's retired.
_X_ (7) No, for some other reason
_X_ (8) I have no mother.

91. Please write the name of your mother's job in this space, along with a few words describing what she does in her job.

_X_ Unemployed or housewife (as coded by me)

92. How much time during the past three years has your mother been out of work *because she could not find a job?*
____ (1) None at all
_X_ (2) Less than six months
_X_ (3) 6 months–1 year
_X_ (4) 1 year–2 years
_X_ (5) More than two years

____ (6) I have no mother.
____ (7) Don't know

XIII

Success of performance in school

	(1) Strongly Agree	(2) Agree	(3) Undecided	(4) Disagree	(5) Strongly Disagree
3. I've had more difficulty doing well in school than most people my age.	0	0	0	1	2

8. What kind of work have teachers expected from you?
   - 2 (1) Excellent work
   - 1 (2) Good work
   - 0 (3) Average work
   - 0 (4) Fair work
   - 0 (5) Poor work
   - 0 (6) No kind of work in particular

9. What has been your most common grade in school?
   - 2 (1) A
   - 1 (2) B
   - 0 (3) C
   - 0 (4) D
   - 0 (5) We don't get letter grades.

10. Do you feel like you've been a success in school?
    - 0 (1) Never
    - 0 (2) Seldom
    - 0 (3) Sometimes
    - 1 (4) Usually
    - 2 (5) Always

XIV

Susceptibility to peer influence

69. Are you ever talked into doing things by your friends that you really don't want to do?
   - 4 (1) Frequently
   - 3 (2) Sometimes
   - 2 (3) Seldom
   - 1 (4) Never

Notes

Chapter 1. Major theoretical perspectives on juvenile delinquency

1 The questioning of the role of social class, based on self-report techniques, will be discussed at length in Chapter 2.

Chapter 3. Tying the pieces together

1 The reader is referred to the section in Chapter 2 dealing with the family for empirical support for this contention.

2 In the diagramming conventions to be utilized throughout this work, the X_i below each construct refers to the presumed causal ordering of the variables, with the lower i being the causally prior. The double (⇒) and single (→) arrows represent the expected relative magnitudes of the causal effects, with double paths carrying the greater theoretical impact.

3 See Chapter 2, the section on the family, for a more complete discussion of the extent to which parental deviance may reverse the effects of parental love or attachment to parents on delinquent behavior. It seems to be very slight.

4 It should be noted that, in causal sequence, strain (X_5) is numbered after parent attachment (X_4), ruling out a priori a causal influence of strain upon parent attachment. The remaining possibility – that parent attachment influences strain – will of course be checked against the data but is presumed to have no particularly significant effects.

5 The argument of middle-class bias can be used to posit a white bias by schools and therefore an eventual higher rate of black and other minority group delinquent behavior. Harvey and Slatin (1975) found that more was expected from whites than blacks in all perceived SES levels.

6 That no other direct causes of delinquent behavior are yet postulated is very significant when one considers the inclusion of such popular "causes" as class and strain in the model.

7 Interestingly, Hirschi places delinquent values in the stake-in-conformity box as "belief in the moral validity of norms." But by the logic of a strict control approach, they can also be placed as a third, spuriously correlated result of prior stakes in conformity (parent and school ties). Why, then, cannot delinquent associates also be transposed to the left or causal side of the model, providing a stake in conformity to the degree the adolescent's friends are nondelinquent?

8 See, for example, Deutscher (1966), Wicker (1969), and Albrecht and Carpenter (1976), for various viewpoints on the complex relationship between attitudes and behavior.

9 The safety-in-numbers phenomenon is consistent with the notion of "risky shift" – the finding that a group seems to be willing to take greater risks than are the individuals who make up the group. See Malamuth and Feshbach (1972) for a more complete discussion.

10 Although the matter is beyond the scope of this study, the feedbacks of extensive and/or official delinquency seem to affect the chances of future deviance mainly through these

same theoretical constructs, i.e., by altering attachments, generating negative attitudes, and almost forcing association with delinquent peers.

11 Hewitt adds the possibility that failure in school can cause a child to turn to parents as well as peers for a greater sense of self-worth. This would be represented by a negative effect of school performance on attachment to parents.

Chapter 4. Methods and measures

1 Of the remaining nonrespondent sophomores, about one-half were absent from school and one-half had schedules that did not include the "required" course in which the questionnaire was administered. Further details of all data-gathering procedures are available from the author.

2 See the Appendix for details of the operationalization of this and all other theoretical constructs, including the actual questionnaire items and the scoring procedures.

3 Only eighteen students failed to respond and were excluded from the pool by default.

4 "And" was not used here because nonresponse to these items was quite substantial, and its use would cause the loss of too many of the dwindling underclass simply by default.

5 Several of the items are in fact borrowed from Nye or from Hirschi (1969). Scoring will be similar for later items, but more detail is included in the text for parent-related items by way of example. In later sections the reader will be asked to depend more on the Appendix for scoring of index items.

6 Such correlations between rotated factors must not be taken too literally, as "some methods tend to make the resulting factors more correlated than others" (Nie et al., 1975:386). Furthermore, the interfactor correlations would decrease if only the items composing the final indexes were included in a factor analysis, as several items were dropped because they failed to load on just one dimension.

7 This procedure is used for all additive indexes unless otherwise stated.

8 See the section on strain in the Appendix for the exact data-gathering devices described in this section of the text.

9 Many self-report studies ask for a recollection of activities during the past three years or "ever," surely an unrealistic request to impose upon the mind of an adolescent filling out a form.

10 This figure is raised from the more common two-dollar level of past studies to counter the effect of inflation.

Chapter 5. Analyzing the results

1 Standardized path coefficients are most useful for analyzing the relative effects of different variables within a given population (see Blalock, 1967). The standardized path coefficient p_{ij} is interpretable as the standard deviation change in the dependent variable *i* (+ or −) for each standard deviation change in the designated variable *j if* all other variables (including residuals) are held constant (cf. Land, 1969). Alternatively, p_{ij} equals the *un*standardized regression coefficient b_{ij} times the ratio of variances (δ_j/δ_i). Thus the standardized path coefficient is determined by effects and variability, which is why unstandardized coefficients will be used in cross-sample comparisons. Finally, the squared path coefficient (p^2_{ij}) represents the proportion of the variance of *i* for which *j* is directly responsible. *Total* effects of *j* on *i* include indirect paths as well.

2 The usual assumptions of multiple regression include assumptions of linear relations, interval scales, homoscedasticity (equal variances), no multicollinearity, normality of condi-

tional distributions of *y* values for a given set of *x* values, and (technically) perfect measurement.

3 Schoenberg (1975:50–2, 147–9), for example, demonstrates with simulations that heteroscedasticity, nonnormality, nonlinearity, and ordinality do not seriously alter the parameter estimates of selected structural models. Hindelang (1971*b*) supports the proposition that the nonnormal distribution of deviant acts does not create too serious problems for statistical analysis. And Labovitz (1967, 1970) and Boyle (1970) show that assuming an underlying metric and assigning arbitrary interval values to ordinal data (which are consistent with the rank order) will rarely alter the results of statistical analysis to an appreciable degree.

4 "Listwise" deletion of missing data is employed throughout the regression runs. That is, a missing value for *any* measure eliminates the respondent from the entire run. This procedure ensures that all coefficients are estimated on the basis of the same sample – a crucial consideration in examining the relative roles of variables. In "pairwise" deletion of missing data, a missing value for a particular variable causes that case to be eliminated from calculations involving that variable only. This procedure results in different coefficients being based on different cases, and "little confidence can be placed in multiple regression statistics when pairwise deletion is used" (Nie et al., 1975:353). Selection of analysis techniques always seems to entail compromise, however, as the choice of listwise deletion sometimes creates quite a substantial reduction in sample size. Moreover, there is the possibility that those remaining in the sample, by virtue of having completed more questionnaire items, may differ somewhat from those excluded (in verbal ability, school attachment, or whatever is related to completing questionnaire items). However, completing versus failing to complete the questionnaire is not significantly related ($p < .01$) to school success, school attachment, delinquent behavior, or any other variable in the model.

5 Standardized path coefficients will be signified by "$p =$" in the text. This should not be confused with levels of statistical significance $p <$ or with unstandardized regression coefficients $b =$.

6 The coefficients shown in Figure 5.2 were obtained in the following manner: All possible effects were tested for significance at the $p < .01$ level. Then the regressions were run again with only those variables with significant effects included in each equation. The paths represented by arrows in Figure 5.2 are those that met the $p < .01$ criterion in the initial run and also met a $p < .05$ significant level in the run limited to significant regressions.

This procedure was followed in all runs labeled as employing a $p < .01$ significance level. For those labeled as $p < .05$, paths had to remain significant beyond $p < .10$ after the elimination of nonsignificant regressions based on $p < .05$ in the initial run. For the few runs (with small sample sizes) labeled as using a $p < .20$ criterion level, that same degree of significance was again required for the path to be retained in the figure after the initial elimination of chance effects.

One important result of including only significant paths in the regression runs reported in the text is that the explained variance (R^2) of the dependent variables does not capitalize on chance explanation from originally insignificant effects. The reported R^2s are therefore conservative estimates that deserve serious attention.

7 When coefficients are interpreted as "high" or "low" in the path diagrams, the reference is to the magnitude *relative* to other coefficients in the same model. In absolute terms, very few coefficients are high, but there is every reason to believe that the "true" parameters have been uniformly attenuated rather than inflated by research procedures.

8 No nonsignificant (not shown in Figure 5.1) path coefficient leading to susceptibility to peer influence exceeded a magnitude of .06.

9 The total effects of the parent–child connection on delinquent behavior shown in Figure 5.3 sum to $p = -.11$.

10 It should be noted that the sample sizes for Figures 5.2 and 5.4 differ substantially. Specifically, using the occupational-expectations measure decreases the effective sample. But it appears that those failing to respond to this item are not sufficiently different from the remaining students to consider this a different sample. The other portions of the original (Figure 5.2) and Figure 5.4 imply virtually identical causal laws. Hence, different interpretations about strain arise from different measures and not from different samples or variances.

11 However, path analysis in general has severe limitations on detecting interaction effects, unless the presence and nature of those interactions is previously hypothesized. Inserting a whole series of cross-product terms into the equations could be done as an exploratory procedure, but it was not seen as useful in the present analysis.

12 There is another path in Figure 5.5 that did not appear in Figure 5.2. It represents an effect of school attachment on perceived certainty. The path's presence in one case and absence in the other results from one's barely missing and the other's barely meeting the arbitrary significance level criterion and is not substantively meaningful. The (unseen) path coefficient in Figure 5.2 is $p = .10$, compared to $p = .11$ in Figure 5.5.

13 Confining effects to those pictured in Figure 5.2 fails to include all of the nonsignificant components of "total effects," almost all of which are in the expected direction. Including all path coefficients would increase the variation explained by the variables, but at the risk of capitalizing on chance fluctuations. Moreover, the focus throughout the analysis is on the relative magnitudes of effects, rather than on trying to explain a great amount of variation. To do the latter is very difficult, owing to measurement unreliabilities and probably to the way things are in reality. On the other hand, the present explained variance ($R^2 = .27$) compares quite favorably with the results of other attempts to develop causal models of delinquency (cf. Empey and Lubeck, 1971*a*).

14 In addition to being partly lost and partly taken over by school performance, some of the original effects of delinquent associates are also taken over by delinquent values, whose standardized effect on delinquent behavior rises from .23 to .38 with delinquent associates omitted.

15 For one thing, associates are also closer, in terms of stronger effects, to later delinquent behavior.

Chapter 6. Findings across subsamples

1 The greater apparent effects of occupational expectations for males are caused by the arbitrary setting of statistical significance at $p < .05$, with the male coefficient barely attaining significance and the female coefficient just missing significance, rather than by substantively significant differences.

2 The low representation of blacks and Asians also makes it unprofitable to look for interactions by race. Larger samples of Asians and blacks will have to be obtained to explore those possibilities.

3 A discussion of the precise ways in which labeling is said to work is beyond the scope of this study. There are numerous sources that include such discussions (see Cicourel, 1968; Emerson, 1969; Lemert, 1972).

4 The sample sizes are too small and the chance of sampling error too great to justify detailed examination of these runs.

Chapter 7. Origins of juvenile delinquency

1 This list omits susceptibility to peer influence and perceived risk of apprehension. They are not discussed in this context because they were introduced into the model from outside the three major perspectives and because they failed to show significant causal effects.

Appendix. The measuring devices

1 Because the mother-attachment index is exactly parallel, there will be no repeat of those items. The questionnaire location of the corresponding mother-related item is in parentheses given directly below the location of number of each father item. The overall attachment-to-parents score is the greater of the mother- or father-attachment scores.
2 This response makes the *entire* index score equal zero.
3 Asterisked responses make the *entire* index score equal zero throughout this section on future-oriented perceived strain.
4 Because the mother-love index is exactly parallel, there will be no repeat of those items. The questionnaire location of the corresponding mother item is given in parentheses directly below the location number of each father item. The overall parental-love score is the greater of the mother- or father-love scores.

References

Ageton, Suzanne S. and Delbert S. Elliott, 1974. "The Effects of Legal Processing on Delinquent Orientations." *Social Problems* 22 (October):87-100.

Akers, Ronald L., 1964. "Socio-Economic Status and Delinquent Behavior: A Retest." *Journal of Research in Crime and Delinquency* 1 (January):38-46.

1973. *Deviant Behavior: A Social Learning Approach.* Belmont, Calif.: Wadsworth.

Albrecht, Stan L. and Kerry E. Carpenter, 1976. "Attitudes as Predictors of Behavior versus Behavior Intentions: A Convergence of Research Traditions." *Sociometry* 39:1-10.

Andenaes, Johannes, 1966. "The General Preventive Effects of Punishment." *University of Pennsylvania Law Review* 114 (May):949-83.

1975. "General prevention Revisited: Research and Policy Implications." *Journal of Criminal Law and Criminology* 66 (September):338-65.

Antunes, G. and A. L. Hunt, 1973. "The Impact of Certainty and Severity of Punishment on Levels of Crime in American States: An Extended Analysis." *Journal of Criminal Law, Criminology and Police Science* 64 (December):486-93.

Arnold, William R., 1965. "Continuities in Research: Scaling Delinquent Behavior." *Social Problems* 13 (Summer):59-66.

Bailey, William, 1976. "Certainty of Arrest and Crime Rates for Major Felonies: A Research Note." *Journal of Research in Crime and Delinquency* 13 (July):145-54.

Bailey, William, J. David Martin, and Louis N. Gray, 1974. "Crime and Deterrence: A Correlation Analysis." *Journal of Research in Crime and Delinquency* 11 (July):124-143.

Bailey, William C. and Ruth P. Lott, 1976. "Crime, Punishment and Personality: An Examination of the Deterrence Question." *Journal of Criminal Law and Criminology* 67 (March): 99-109.

Bandura, Albert and Richard H. Walters, 1959. *Adolescent Aggression.* New York: Ronald Press.

Bean, F. D. and R. G. Cushing, 1971. "Criminal Homicide, Punishment, and Deterrence: Methodological and Substantive Reconsiderations." *Social Science Quarterly* 52 (September): 277-89.

Beccaria, C. 1764. *On Crimes and Punishments.* Trans. by H. Paolucci, 1963. Indianapolis: Bobbs-Merrill.

Bedau, H. A. 1970. "Deterrence and the Death Penalty: A Reconsideration." *Journal of Criminal Law, Criminology and Police Science* 61 (December):539-48.

Bentham, J., 1830. *The Rationale of Punishment.* London: R. Heward.

Berger, Alan S. and William Simon, 1974. "Black families and the Moynihan Report: A Research Evaluation." *Social Problems* 22 (December):145-61.

Berman, Gerald S. and Marie R. Haug, 1975. "Occupational and Educational Goals and Expectations: The Effects of Race and Sex." *Social Problems* 23 (December):166-81.

Blackmore, John, 1974. "The Relationship between Self-reported Delinquency and Official Convictions Amongst Adolescent Boys." *British Journal of Criminology* 14 (April): 172-6.

Blalock, Hubert M., Jr., 1961. "Evaluating the Relative Importance of Variables." *American Sociological Review* 26 (December):866–74.

1967. "Path Coefficients vs. Regression Coefficients." *American Journal of Sociology* 72 (May):675–6.

1972. *Social Statistics* (2nd edn). New York: McGraw-Hill.

Blau, Peter M., 1957. "Occupational Bias and Mobility." *American Sociological Review* 22 (August):392–9.

Bloch, Herbert A., 1963. "The Juvenile Gang: A Cultural Reflex." *Annals of the American Academy of Political and Social Science* 347 (May):20–9.

Bloch, Herbert A. and Arthur Niederhoffer, 1958. *The Gang: A Study of Adolescent Behavior.* New York: Philosophical Library.

Bohlke, Robert H., 1961. "Social Mobility, Stratification Inconsistency and Middle Class Delinquency." *Social Problems* 8 (Spring):351–63.

Bohrnstedt, George W. and T. M. Carter, 1971. "Robustness in Regression Analysis," in H. L. Costner (ed.), *Sociological Methodology,* pp. 118–46. San Francisco: Jossey-Bass.

Boyle, R. P., 1970. "Path Analysis and Ordinal Data." *American Journal of Sociology* 75 (January):461–80.

Braun, Carl, 1976. "Teacher Expectation: Sociopsychological Dynamics." *Review of Educational Research* 46:185–213.

Briar, Scott and Irving Piliavin, 1965. "Delinquency, Situational Inducements, and Commitment to Conformity." *Social Problems* 13 (Summer): 35–45.

California Assembly Office of Research, 1968. *Crime and Penalties in California.*

Campbell, D. T. and H. L. Ross, 1968. "The Connecticut Crackdown on Speeding: Time-Series Data in Quasi-Experimental Analysis." *Law and Society Review* 3 (August):33–53.

Caro, Francis G. and C. Terance Pihlblad, 1965. "Aspirations and Expectations: A Re-examination of the Bases for Social Class Differences in the Occupational Orientation of Male High School Students." *Sociology and Social Research* 49:465–75.

Carter, Robert M., 1968. *Middle-Class Delinquency: An Experiment in Community Control.* Berkeley: University of California, School of Criminology.

Chambliss, W. J., 1966. "The Deterrent Influence of Punishment." *Crime and Delinquency* 12 (January): 70–5.

Chiricos, T. and G. Waldo, 1970. "Punishment and Crime: An Examination of Some Empirical Evidence." *Social Problems* 18 (Fall):200–17.

Cicourel, Aaron V., 1968. *The Social Organization of Juvenile Justice.* New York: Wiley.

Clark, John P. and L. L. Tifft, 1966. "Polygraph and Interview Validation of Self-reported Deviant Behavior." *American Sociological Review* 31:516–23.

Clark, John P. and Eugene P. Wenninger, 1962. "Socio-economic Class and Area as Correlates of Illegal Behavior among Juveniles." *American Sociological Review* 27 (December): 826–34.

1963. "Goal Orientations and Illegal Behavior among Juveniles." *Social Forces* 42 (October): 49–59.

Claster, D. S., 1967. "Comparisons of Risk Perception between Delinquents and Non-delinquents." *Journal of Criminal Law, Criminology and Police Science* 58 (March): 80–6.

Clay, Daniel C., 1976. "Parent-Child Rapport: An Important Factor in the Structuring of Educational Ambition in Rural America." Paper presented at the annual meeting of the Rural Sociological Society, New York.

Cloward, Richard A. and Lloyd E. Ohlin, 1960. *Delinquency and Opportunity.* New York: Free Press.

Cohen, Albert K., 1955. *Delinquent Boys.* Glencoe, Ill.: Free Press.

Conger, Rand D., 1976. "Social Control and Social Learning Models of Delinquent Behavior: A Synthesis." *Criminology* 14 (May):17–40.

Datesman, Susan K., Frank R. Scrapitti, and Richard M. Stephenson, 1975. "Female Delinquency: An Application of Self and Opportunity Theories." *Journal of Research in Crime and Delinquency* 12 (July):107–23.

Dentler, Robert A. and Lawrence J. Monroe, 1961. "Social Correlates of Early Adolescent Theft." *American Sociological Review* 26 (October):733–43.

Deutsch, Martin (ed.), 1967. *The Disadvantaged Child.* New York: Basic Books.

Deutscher, Irwin, 1966. "Words and Deeds: Social Science and Social Policy." *Social Problems* 13 (Winter):235–54.

Douglas, J. W. B., J. M. Ross, W. A. Hammond, and D. G. Mulligan, 1966. "Delinquency and Social Class." *British Journal of Criminology* 6 (July):294–302.

Downes, David M., 1966. *The Delinquent Solution.* New York: Free Press.

Ehrlich, I., 1973. "Participation in Illegitimate Activities: A Theoretical and Empirical Investigation." *Journal of Political Economy* 81 (May–June):521–65.

Elliott, Delbert S., 1961. "Delinquency, Opportunity, and Patterns of Orientations." Unpublished doctoral dissertation, University of Washington, Seattle.

1962. "Delinquency and Perceived Opportunity." *Sociological Inquiry* 32 (Spring):216–27.

Elliott, Delbert S., and Harwin L. Voss, 1974. *Delinquency and Dropout.* Lexington, Mass: Lexington Books.

Emerson, Robert M., 1969. *Judging Delinquents: Context and Process in Juvenile Court.* Chicago: Aldine Publishing Co.

Empey, Lamar T., 1956. "Social Class and Occupational Aspirations: A Comparison of Absolute and Relative Measurement." *American Sociological Review* 21 (December):703–9.

1967. "Delinquency Theory and Recent Research." *Journal of Research in Crime and Delinquency* 4 (January):28–42.

Empey, Lamar T. and Steven G. Lubeck, 1971*a*. *Explaining Delinquency: Construction, Test, and Reformulation of a Sociological Theory.* Lexington, Mass: Heath Lexington Books.

1971*b*. *The Silverlake Experiment.* Chicago: Aldine Publishing Co.

England, Ralph W., Jr., 1960. "A Theory of Middle Class Juvenile Delinquency." *Journal of Criminal Law, Criminology and Police Science* 50 (March–April):535–40.

Epstein, Norman, 1967. "Delinquent Interactions between Middle Class Adolescents and Their Parents." *Juvenile Court Judges Journal* 17 (Winter):135–8.

Erickson, Maynard L., 1972. "The Changing Relationship between Official and Self-reported Measures of Delinquency: An Exploratory–Predictive Study." *Journal of Criminal Law, Criminology and Police Science* 63 (September):388–95.

1973. "Group Violations, SES, and Official Delinquency." *Social Forces* 52 (September): 41–52.

Erickson, Maynard L. and Lamar T. Empey, 1965. "Class Position, Peers, and Delinquency." *Sociology and Social Research* 49 (April):268–82.

Erickson, Maynard L. and Jack P. Gibbs, 1976. "Further Findings on the Deterrence Question and Strategies for Future Research." *Journal of Criminal Justice* 4 (Fall):175–90.

Erickson, Maynard L., Jack P. Gibbs, and Gary F. Jensen, 1977. "The Deterrence Doctrine and the Perceived Certainty of Legal Punishments." *American Sociological Review* 42 (April):305–17.

Erickson, Maynard L. and W. B. Smith, 1974. "On the Relationship between Self-reported and Actual Deviance." *Humbolt Journal of Social Relations* 2 (Spring/Summer):106–13.

Farrington, David P., 1973. "Self-reports of Deviant Behavior: Predictive and Stable?" *Journal of Criminal Law and Criminology* 64 (March):99–110.

Fisher, Gene A. and Maynard L. Erickson, 1973. "On Assessing the Effects of Official Reactions to Juvenile Delinquency." *Journal of Research in Crime and Delinquency* 10 (July): 177–94.

Fisher, Sethard, 1972. "Stigma and Deviant Careers in School." *Social Problems* 20 (Summer): 78–83.

Foster, Jack D., Simon Dinitz, and Walter C. Reckless, 1972. "Perceptions of Stigma Following Public Intervention for Delinquent Behavior." *Social Problems* 20 (Fall): 202–9.

Frease, Dean E., 1973. "Delinquency, Social Class, and the Schools." *Sociology and Social Research* 57 (July): 443–59.

Fredericks, Marcel A. and Martin Molnar, 1969. "Relative Occupational Anticipations and Aspirations of Delinquents and Nondelinquents." *Journal of Research in Crime and Delinquency* 6 (January): 1–7.

Friday, Paul C. and Jerald Hage, 1976. "Youth Crime in Postindustrial Societies: An Integrated Perspective." *Criminology* 14 (November): 347–68.

Gibbens, T. C. N. and R. H. Ahrenfeldt, 1966. *Cultural Factors in Delinquency*. Philadelphia: J. B. Lippincott.

Gibbons, Don C., 1976. *Delinquent Behavior* (2nd edn). Englewood Cliffs, N.J.: Prentice-Hall.

Gibbs, Jack P., 1968. "Crime, Punishment, and Deterrence." *Social Science Quarterly* 48 (March): 515–30.

1975. *Crime Punishment and Deterrence*. New York: Elsevier.

Glaser, Daniel, Bernard Lander, and William Abbott, 1971. "Opiate Addicted and Non-addicted Siblings in a Slum Area." *Social Problems* 18 (Spring): 510–21.

Glueck, Sheldon and Eleanor Glueck, 1950. *Unraveling Juvenile Delinquency*. Cambridge, Mass.: Harvard University Press.

Gold, Martin, 1963. *Status Forces in Delinquent Boys*. Ann Arbor: Institute for Social Research, University of Michigan.

1966. "Undetected Delinquent Behavior." *Journal of Research in Crime and Delinquency* 3 (January): 27–46.

Gold, Martin and Harwin L. Voss, 1967. "On Social Status and Delinquency: Communications by: Martin Gold, Harwin L. Voss." *Social Problems* 15 (Summer): 114–22.

Gold, Martin and Jay R. Williams, 1969. "The Effect of Getting Caught: Apprehension of a Juvenile Offender as a Cause of Subsequent Delinquencies." *Prospectus* 3 (December): 1–12.

Gordon, Robert A., 1968. "Issues in Multiple Regression." *American Journal of Sociology* 73: 592–616.

Gould, L. C., 1969. "Who Defines Delinquency: A Comparison of Self-reported and Officially Reported Indices of Delinquency for Three Racial Groups." *Social Problems* 16 (Spring): 325–36.

Gray, L. and J. D. Martin, 1969. "Punishment and Deterrence: Another Analysis of Gibbs' Data." *Social Science Quarterly* 49 (September): 389–95.

Hall, Vernon C., John W. Huppertz, and Alan Levi, 1977. "Attention and Achievement Exhibited by Middle- and Lower-Class Black and White Elementary School Boys." *Journal of Educational Psychology* 69 (April): 115–20.

Haney, William and Martin Gold, 1973. "The Juvenile Delinquent Nobody Knows." *Psychology Today* 7 (September): 48–55.

Hanson, Ralph A., 1975. "Consistency and Stability of Home Environmental Measures Related to IQ." *Child Development* 46 (June): 470–80.

Hardt, Robert H. and George E. Bodine, 1965. *Development of Self-report Instruments in Delinquency Research*. Syracuse, N.Y.: Syracuse University Youth Development Center.

Hardt, Robert H. and Sandra Peterson-Hardt, 1977. "On Determining the Quality of the Delinquency Self-report Method." *Journal of Research in Crime and Delinquency* 14 (July): 247–61.

Harvey, Dale G. and Gerald T. Slatin, 1975. "The Relationship between Child's SES and Teacher Expectations: A Test of the Middle-Class Bias Hypothesis. *Social Forces* 54 (September):140–59.

Heller, Celia S. 1969. *Structured Social Inequality.* London: Macmillan.

Hepburn, John R., 1976. "Testing Alternative Models of Delinquency Causation." *Journal of Criminal Law and Criminology* 67 (December):450–60.

Hewitt, John P., 1970. *Social Stratification and Deviant Behavior.* New York: Random House.

Himelhoch, Jerome, 1964. "Socio-Economic Status and Delinquency in Rural New England." Paper presented at the annual meeting of the American Sociological Association, Montreal.

Hindelang, Michael J., 1970. "The Commitment of Delinquents to Their Misdeeds: Do Delinquents Drift?" *Social Problems* 17 (Spring):502–9.

1971*a*. "Age, Sex, and the Versatility of Delinquent Involvements." *Social Problems* 18 (Spring):522–35.

1971*b*. "The Effects of Normality Violations on the Interpretation of Correlation Coefficients." *Journal of Research in Crime and Delinquency* 8 (July):156–64.

1973. "Causes of Delinquency: A Partial Replication and Extension." *Social Problems* 20 (Spring):471–87.

1974. "Moral Evaluations and Illegal Behaviors." *Social Problems* 21 (February):370–85.

Hirschi, Travis, 1969. *Causes of Delinquency.* Berkeley: University of California Press.

Hirschi, Travis and Michael Hindelang, 1977. "Intelligence and Delinquency: A Revisionist Review." *American Sociological Review* 42 (August):571–86.

Hirschi, Travis and Hanan C. Selvin, 1966. "False Criteria of Causality in Delinquency Research." *Social Problems* 13 (Winter):254–68.

Hood, Roger and Richard Sparks, 1970, *Key Issues in Criminology.* New York: McGraw-Hill.

Jenkins, Richard L., 1957. "Motivation and Frustration in Delinquency." *American Journal of Orthopsychiatry* 27 (July):528–37.

Jensen, Gary F., 1969. " 'Crime Doesn't Pay': Correlates of a Shared Misunderstanding." *Social Problems* 17 (Fall):189–201.

1972. "Parents, Peers, and Delinquent Action: A Test of the Differential Association Perspective." *American Journal of Sociology* 78 (November):562–75.

1973. "Inner Containment and Delinquency." *Journal of Criminal Law and Criminology* 64 (December):464–70.

Jensen, Gary F. and Raymond Eve, 1976. "Sex Differences in Delinquency: An Examination of Popular Sociological Explanations." *Criminology* 13 (February):427–48.

Jessor, Richard, Theodore D. Ceraves, Robert C. Hanson, and Shirley L. Jessor, 1968. *Society, Personality, and Deviant Behavior: A Study of a Tri-Ethnic Community.* New York: Holt, Rinehart and Winston.

Johnson, Richard E., 1972. "The Relevance of Social Class in the Causation of Delinquency." Unpublished master's thesis. University of Washington, Seattle.

1973. "Theory of Processes Leading to Delinquent Involvement." Unpublished manuscript.

1974. "Deterrence." Unpublished "Analytic Specialty." University of Washington Sociology Department, Seattle.

Kandle, Robert J., 1974. "Perceived Risk as Deterrence: Some New Evidence Bearing on an Old Question." Unpublished master's thesis. University of Washington, Seattle.

Karacki, Larry and Jackson Toby, 1962. "The Uncommitted Adolescent: Candidate for Gang Socialization." *Sociological Inquiry* 22 (Spring):203–15.

Kelly, Delos H. and William T. Pink, 1973. "School Commitment, Youth Rebellion, and Delinquency." *Criminology* 10 (February):473-85.

1975. "Status Origins, Youth Rebellion, and Delinquency: A Reexamination of the Class Issue." *Journal of Youth and Adolescence* 4 (December):339-47.

Kerckhoff, Alan C. and Judith L. Huff, 1974. "Parental Influence on Educational Goals." *Sociometry* 37:307-27.

Kim, Jae-On, 1975. "Multivariate Analysis of Ordinal Variables." *American Journal of Sociology* 81 (September):261-98.

Kim, Jae-On and Frank J. Kohout, 1975. "Special Topics in General Linear Models," in Norman H. Nie et al., *Statistical Package for the Social Sciences* (2nd edn), pp. 368-97. New York: McGraw-Hill.

Kluckhohn, Florence and Fred L. Strodtbeck, 1973. *Variation in Value Orientation.* Westport, Conn.: Greenwood Press.

Kobrin, Solomon, 1951. "The Conflict of Values in Delinquency Areas." *American Sociological Review* 16 (October):653-61.

Kohn, Melvin, 1969. *Class and Conformity.* Homewood, Ill.: Dorsey Press.

Kvaraceus, William C. and Walter B. Miller, 1959. *Delinquent Behavior: Culture and the Individual.* Washington, D.C.: National Education Association.

Kvaraceus, William C. and William E. Ulrich, 1959. *Delinquent Behavior: Principles and Practices.* Washington, D.C.: National Education Association.

Labovitz, Sanford, 1967. "Some Observations on Measurement and Statistics." *Social Forces* 46 (December):151-60.

1970. "The Assignment of Numbers to Rank Order Categories." *American Sociological Review* 35 (June):515-24.

Land, Kenneth C., 1969. "Principles of Path Analysis," in Edgar F. Borgotta and George W. Bohrnstedt (eds.), *Sociological Methodology,* pp. 3-37. San Francisco: Jossey-Bass.

Landis, J., S. Dinitz, and W. Reckless, 1963. "Implementing Two Theories of Delinquency: Value Orientations and Awareness of Limited Opportunity." *Sociology and Social Research* 47 (July):404-16.

Lemert, Edwin M., 1972. "The Concept of Secondary Deviation," in E. M. Lemert, *Human Deviance, Social Problems, and Social Control* (2nd edn), pp. 62-92. Englewood Cliffs, N.J.: Prentice-Hall.

Lerman, Paul, 1968. "Individual Values, Peer Values, and Subcultural Delinquency." *American Sociological Review* 33 (April):760-73.

Lesieur, Henry R. and Peter M. Lehman, 1975. "Remeasuring Delinquency: A Replication and Critique." *British Journal of Criminology* 15 (January):69-80.

Linden, Eric W., 1974. "Interpersonal Ties and Delinquent Behavior." Unpublished doctoral dissertation. University of Washington, Seattle.

Linden, Eric and James C. Hackler, 1973. "Affective Ties and Delinquency." *Pacific Sociological Review* 16 (January):27-46.

Liska, Allen E., 1971. "Aspirations, Expectations, and Delinquency: Stress and Additive Models." *Sociological Quarterly* 12 (Winter):99-106.

1973. "Delinquency Involvement and Delinquent Peers." *Sociology and Social Research* 58 (October):23-36.

1974. "Emergent Issues in the Attitude-Behavior Consistency Controversy." *American Sociological Review* 39 (April):261-72.

Logan, C. H., 1972. "General Deterrent Effects of Imprisonment." *Social Forces* 51 (September):64-73.

Love, Leonore R. and Jaques W. Kaswan, 1974. *Troubled Children: Their Families, Schools, and Treatments.* New York: Wiley.

McClelland, David C., John W. Atkinson, Russell A. Clark, and Edgar L. Lowell, 1953. *The Achievement Motive.* New York: Appleton-Century-Crofts.

Maccoby, Eleanor E., J. P. Johnson, and R. M. Church, 1958. "Community Integration and the Social Control of Juvenile Delinquency." *Journal of Social Issues* 14 (No. 3): 38–51.

McCord, Joan and William McCord, 1964. "The Effects of Parental Role Model on Criminality," in Ruth Shonle Cavan (ed.), *Readings in Juvenile Delinquency,* pp. 170–80. Philadelphia: J. B. Lippincott.

McDonald, Lynn, 1969. *Social Class and Delinquency.* London: Faber and Faber.

McKinley, Donald G., 1964. *Social Class and Family Life.* New York: Free Press.

Malamuth, N. and S. Feshbach, 1972. "Risky Shift in a Naturalistic Setting." *Journal of Personality* 40 (March): 38–49.

Matza, David, 1964. *Delinquency and Drift.* New York: Wiley.

1969. *Becoming Deviant.* Englewood Cliffs, N.J.: Prentice-Hall.

Matza, David and G. Sykes, 1961. "Juvenile Delinquency and Subterranean Values." *American Sociological Review* 26 (October):712-19.

Mayer, Kurt B., 1963. "The Changing Shape of the American Class Structure." *Social Research* 30 (Winter): 458–68.

Merton, Robert K., 1938. "Social Structure and Anomie." *American Sociological Review* 3 (October):672–82.

Miller, Dorothy, Ann Rosenthal, Don Miller, and Sheryl Ruzek, 1971. "Public Knowledge of Criminal Penalties: A Research Report," in S. E. Grupp (ed.), *Theories of Punishment,* pp. 205–26. Bloomington, Ind.: Indiana University Press.

Miller, Jerome G., 1970. "Research and Theory in Middle-Class Delinquency." *British Journal of Criminology* 10 (January):33–51.

Miller, Patricia Y. and William Simon, 1974. "Adolescent Sexual Behavior: Context and Change. *Social Problems* 22 (October): 58–76.

Miller, Walter B., 1958. "Lower Class Culture as a Generating Milieu of Gang Delinquency." *Journal of Social Issues* 14 (no. 3):5–19.

Mills, C. Wright, 1951. *White Collar.* New York: Oxford University Press.

Mortimer, Jeylan T., 1976. "Social Class, Work and the Family: Some Implications of the Father's Occupation for Familial Relationships and Sons' Career Decisions." *Journal of Marriage and the Family* 38 (May):241–56.

Mueller, B. Jeanne, 1974. "Rural Family Life Style and Sons' School Achievement." *Rural Sociology* 39: 362–72.

Murphy, Fred J., Mary M. Shirley, and Helen L. Witmer, 1946. "The Incidence of Hidden Delinquency." *American Journal of Orthopsychiatry* 16 (October): 686–95.

Murphy, James, 1974. "Teacher Expectations and Working-Class Under-Achievement." *British Journal of Sociology* 25: 326–44.

Nie, Norman H., C. Hadlai Hull, Jean G. Jenkins, Karin Steinbrenner, and Dale H. Bent, 1975. *Statistical Package for the Social Sciences* (2nd edn). New York: McGraw-Hill.

Nye, F. Ivan, 1958. *Family Relationships and Delinquent Behavior.* New York: Wiley.

Nye, F. Ivan and James F. Short, Jr., 1956. "Scaling Delinquent Behavior." *American Sociological Review* 22 (June): 326–31.

Nye, F. Ivan, James F. Short, Jr., and Virgil J. Olson, 1958. "Socio-Economic Status and Delinquent Behavior." *American Journal of Sociology* 63 (January):381–9.

Palmer, Jan, 1977. "Economic Analysis of the Deterrent Effect of Punishment: A Review." *Journal of Research in Crime and Delinquency* 14 (January):4–21.

Parsons, Talcott, 1947. "Certain Primary Sources and Patterns of Aggression in the Social Structure of the Western World." *Psychiatry* 10 (May): 167–81.

Pine, Gerald J., 1965. "Social Class, Social Mobility, and Delinquent Behavior." *Personnel and Guidance Journal* 43 (April): 770–4.

Polk, Kenneth, 1971. "A Reassessment of Middle-Class Delinquency." *Youth and Society* 2 (March): 333–53.

Polk, Kenneth and D. Halferty, 1966. "Adolescence, Commitment, and Delinquency." *Journal of Research in Crime and Delinquency* 4 (July): 82-96.

Porterfield, Austin L., 1943. "Delinquency and Its Outcome in Court and College." *American Journal of Sociology* 49 (November): 199-208.

Porterfield, Austin L. and Stanley C. Clifton, 1946. *Youth in Trouble.* Fort Worth: Leo Potishmen Foundation.

President's Commission on Law Enforcement and Administration of Justice, 1967. *The Challenge of Crime in a Free Society.* Washington, D.C.: U.S. Government Printing Office.

Quicker, John C., 1974. "The Effect of Goal Discrepancy on Delinquency." *Social Problems* 22 (October): 76-86.

Rehberg, Richard A. and Evelyn Rosenthal, 1975. "Social Class and Its Comparative Impact on a Set of Selected School Process Variables at the High School Level: A Multi-study Analysis. Working Draft." Paper presented at the annual meeting of American Educational Research Association, Washington, D.C.

Reiss, Albert J., Jr., O.D. Duncan, P. K. Hatt, and C. C. North, 1961. *Occupations and Social Status.* New York: Free Press of Glencoe.

Reiss, Albert J., Jr. and Albert Lewis Rhodes, 1961. "The Distribution of Juvenile Delinquency in the Social Class Structure." *American Sociological Review* 26 (October): 720-32;

1963. "Status Deprivation and Delinquent Behavior." *Sociological Quarterly* 4 (Spring): 135–49.

Rinehart, James W., 1971. "Affluence and the Embourgeoisement of the Working Class: A Critical Look." *Social Problems* 19 (Fall): 149-62.

Robinson, W. P., 1975. "Boredom at School." *British Journal of Educational Psychology* 45: 141-52.

Rodman, Hyman, 1963. "The Lower-Class Value Stretch." *Social Forces* 42 (December): 205-15.

Rodman, Hyman, Patricia Voydanoff, and Albert E. Lovejoy, 1974. "The Range of Aspirations: A New Approach." *Social Problems* 22 (December): 184-98.

Rosenthal, Robert, 1973. "The Pygmalion Effect Lives." *Psychology Today* 7 (September): 56-63.

Rosenthal, Robert and Lenore Jacobson, 1968. *Pygmalion in the Classroom.* New York: Holt, Rinehart and Winston.

Rusche, G. and O. Kirchheimer, 1939. *Punishment and Social Structure.* New York: Columbia University Press.

Rushing, William A., 1970. "Class Differences in Goal Orientations and Aspirations: Rural Patterns." *Rural Sociology* 35 (September): 377-95.

Schafer, Walter E. and Kenneth Polk, 1967. "Delinquency and the Schools," in President's Commission on Law Enforcement and Administration of Justice, *Task Force Report: Juvenile Delinquency and Youth Crime,* Appendix M. Washington, D.C.: U.S. Government Printing Office.

Scheussler, Karl F., 1971. "Continuities in Social Prediction," in H. L. Costner (ed.), *Sociological Methodology,* pp. 302-30. San Francisco: Jossey-Bass.

Schoenberg, Ronald J., 1975. "A Structural Model of Delinquency." Unpublished doctoral dissertation. University of Washington, Seattle.

Schrag, Clarence, 1971. *Crime and Justice: American Style.* Washington, D.C.: U.S. Government Printing Office.

Schwartz, B., 1968. "The Effect in Philadelphia of Pennsylvania's Increased Penalties for Rape and Attempted Rape." *Journal of Criminal Law, Criminology and Police Science* 59 (September): 509–15.

Schwendinger, Herman, 1963. "The Instrumental Theory of Delinquency." Unpublished doctoral dissertation. University of California, Los Angeles.

Scott, John Finley, 1959. "Two Dimensions of Delinquent Behavior." *American Sociological Review* 24 (April): 240–3.

Segalman, Ralph, 1965. "The Conflict of Cultures between Social Work and the Underclass." *Rocky Mountain Social Science Journal* 2 (October):161–173.

Sellin, Thorsten and Marvin E. Wolfgang, 1964. *The Measurement of Delinquency.* New York: Wiley.

Shaw, Clifford and Henry D. McKay, 1942. *Juvenile Delinquency in Urban Areas.* Chicago: University of Chicago Press.

Short, James F., Jr. 1964. "Gang Delinquency and Anomie," in M. B. Clinard (ed.), *Anomie and Deviant Behavior,* pp. 98–127. New York: Free Press.

Short, James F., Jr. and F. Ivan Nye, 1957. "Reported Behavior as a Criterion of Deviant Behavior." *Social Problems* 5 (Winter): 207–13.

1958. "Extent of Unrecorded Juvenile Delinquency: Tentative Conclusions." *Journal of Criminal Law, Criminology and Police Science* 49 (November–December): 296–302.

Short, James F., Jr., Ramon Rivera, and Ray A. Tennyson, 1965. "Perceived Opportunities, Gang Membership and Delinquency." *American Sociological Review* 30 (February): 56–67.

Short, James F., Jr. and Fred L. Strodtbeck, 1965. *Group Process and Gang Delinquency.* Chicago: University of Chicago Press.

Siegal, Larry J., Spencer A. Rathus, and Carol Ann Ruppert, 1973. "Values and Delinquency." *British Journal of Criminology* 13 (July): 237–44.

Silberman, Matthew, 1976. "Toward a Theory of Criminal Deterrence." *American Sociological Review* 41 (June):442–61.

Slocum, Walter L. and Carol L. Stone, 1963. "Family Culture Patterns and Delinquent-type Behavior." *Journal of Marriage and Family Living* 25 (May): 202–8.

Spergel, Irving, 1961. "An Exploratory Research in Delinquent Subculture." *Social Service Review* 35 (March): 33–47.

Stinchcombe, Arthur L., 1964. *Rebellion in the High School.* Chicago: Quadrangle Books.

Sutherland, Edwin H., 1949. *White Collar Crime.* New York: Dryden.

Sutherland, Edwin H. and Donald Cressey, 1974. *Criminology* (9th edn). Philadelphia: Lippincott.

Sykes, Gresham M. and David Matza, 1957. "Techniques of Neutralization: A Theory of Delinquency." *American Journal of Sociology* 22 (December): 664–70.

Teevan, James J., Jr., 1976*a*. "Deterrent Effects of Punishment: Subjective Measures Continued." *Canadian Journal of Criminology and Corrections* 18 (April): 152–60.

1976*b*. "Subjective Perception of Deterrence (Continued)." *Journal of Research in Crime and Delinquency* 13 (July): 155–64.

Tittle, Charles R., 1969. "Crime Rates and Legal Sanction." *Social Problems* 16 (Spring):409–23.

1975. Deterrents or Labeling?" *Social Forces* 53 (March):399–410.

Tittle, Charles R. and C. H. Logan, 1973. "Sanctions and Deviance: Evidence and Remaining Questions." *Law and Society Review* 7 (September): 371–92.

Tittle, Charles R. and Alan R. Rowe, 1974. "Certainty of Arrest and Crime Rates: A Further Test of the Deterrence Hypothesis." *Social Forces* 52 (June):455–562.

Toby, Jackson, 1957. "Social Disorganization and Stake in Conformity: Complementary Factors in the Predatory Behavior of Hoodlums." *Journal of Criminal Law, Criminology and Police Science* 48 (May–June): 12–17

1974. "The Socialization and Control of Deviant Motivation," in Daniel Glaser (ed.), *Handbook of Criminology,* pp. 85–100. Chicago: Rand McNally.

Touliatos, John, Byron W. Kinholm, and Amy Rich, 1977. "Interaction of Race with Other Variables on Achievement in School." *Psychology in the Schools* 14 (July): 360–3.

Trotman, Frances Keith, 1977. "Race, IQ, and the Middle Class." *Journal of Educational Psychology* 69 (June):266–73.

U.S. Department of Commerce, Bureau of the Census, 1963. *U.S. Census of the Population: 1960: Subject Reports: Occupational Characteristics.* Final Report PC(2)–7A. Washington, D.C.: U.S. Government Printing Office.

Uzell, Odell, 1961. "Occupational Aspirations of Negro Male High School Students." *Sociology and Social Research* 45 (January):202–4.

Vaz, Edmund W., 1966. "Self-reported Delinquency and Socio-Economic Status." *Canadian Journal of Corrections* 8:20–7.

1967. "Juvenile Delinquency in the Middle Class Culture," in E. W. Vaz (ed.), *Middle Class Juvenile Delinquency,* pp. 131–47. New York: Harper and Row.

Voss, Harwin L., 1966. "Socio-Economic Status and Reported Delinquent Behavior." *Social Problems* 13 (Winter): 314–24.

Voss, Harwin L. (ed.), 1970. *Society, Delinquency, and Delinquent Behavior.* Boston: Little, Brown.

Waldo, G. P. and T. G. Chiricos, 1972. "Perceived Penal Sanction and Self-reported Criminality: A Neglected Approach to Deterrence Research. *Social Problems* 19 (Spring): 522–40.

Watters, James and Nick Stinnett, "Parent Child Relationships: A Decade Review of Research." *Journal of Marriage and the Family* 33 (February): 70–103.

Weis, Joseph G., 1973. "Delinquency among the Well to Do." Unpublished doctoral dissertation. University of California, Berkeley.

Wellford, Charles F. and Michael Wiatrowski, 1975. "On the Measurement of Delinquency." *Journal of Criminal Law and Criminology* 66 (June):175–88.

Wicker, A. W., 1969. "Attitudes vs. Actions: The Relationship of Verbal and Overt Behavior Responses to Attitude Objects." *Journal of Social Issues* 25:41–78.

Wilkins, William E., 1976. "The Concept of a Self-fulfilling Prophecy." *Sociology of Education* 49 (April): 175–83.

Williams, Jay R. and Martin Gold, 1972. "From Delinquent Behavior to Official Delinquency." *Social Problems* 20 (Fall):209–29.

Wilson, T. P., 1970. "Critique of Ordinal Variables." *Social Forces* 49 (March):432–3.

Wise, Nancy Barton, 1967. "Juvenile Delinquency among Middle-Class Girls," in Edmund W. Vaz (ed.), *Middle-class Juvenile Delinquency,* pp. 179–88. New York: Harper and Row.

Wolfgang, Marvin, Robert M. Figlio, and Thorsten Sellin, 1972. *Delinquency in a Birth Cohort.* Chicago: University of Chicago Press.

Zegiob, Leslie E. and Rex Forehand, 1975. "Maternal Interactive Behavior as a Function of Race, Socioeconomic Status, and Sex of the Child." *Child Development* 46:564–8.

Zimring, F. E., 1971. *Crime and Delinquency Issues: Perspectives on Deterrence.* Washington, D.C.: U.S. Government Printing Office.

Zimring, F. E. and G. Hawkins, 1973. *Deterrence: The Legal Threat in Crime Control.* Chicago: University of Chicago Press.

Index